Cat on the Fiddle

A Farcical Comedy

by

JOHN DOLE

Samuel French–London

New York–Sydney–Toronto–Hollywood

Cat on the Fiddle

This play was first produced under the title 'Hot Ice' at the Playhouse, Erith, on 14th September 1963, with the following cast:

DAVID ABBOTT	John Wharton
KATE ABBOTT	Betty Willard
MRS. MACWHIMBLE	Elizabeth McNie
MRS. SCOTT	Betty Cottee
TAXI-DRIVER	Louis Cox
A VISITOR	Kathleen Clark
CUTHBERT FORTESCUE	Tony Stebbings
ARTURO CELLINI	Alex Baird
MRS. BOTTLE	Effie Castleton
TWO POLICEMEN	{ Ted Brooks / John Monk }

The play was directed by T. HADLEY PRESTAGE

with décor by SEAMUS MULCAHY.

The action takes place in the ABBOTTS' *rented flat in London.*

ACT ONE

SCENE 1	An afternoon in spring
SCENE 2	Later the same day

ACT TWO

SCENE 1	That night
SCENE 2	Next morning

ACT THREE

Later the same day

No character in this play is intended to portray any specific person, alive or dead.

NOTE: *The running time of this play, excluding the intervals, is approximately one hour and forty-five minutes.*

PRODUCTION NOTE

This play should be produced as a light-hearted romp at a galloping pace, giving the audience no time to consider the credibility of the various unlikely situations. At the same time the story-line, which is perhaps a little stronger than in many farces, should not be lost in the rush.

The characters are as mixed a bunch as you are likely to find outside the United Nations and provide plenty of opportunities for contrasts of mood and style: contrasts, for example, between Maria's flamboyance and self-possession and David's artless innocence, between Mrs. MacWhimble's narrow-minded bluster and Mrs. Scott's calm assurance. But for all their diversity the characters have one thing in common: however ludicrous the situation they never see the funny side themselves and many of the laughs spring from this paradox.

The audience must be persuaded from the outset to believe in the relationship between David and Kate. The actor and actress playing these parts should convey the close understanding between a happily married couple with their private banter and acceptance of one another's shortcomings. David can be allowed his share of the tomfoolery but should resist any temptation to guy the part. While he is not above taking advantage of the odd situation when it presents itself he is basically a well-intentioned if accident-prone young fellow. He surveys the disastrous results of his handiwork with as much genuine astonishment as if a genie had materialized out of one of his own wine bottles. Kate needs to be played fairly straight and stern but not too heavily. She is no virago, just a loving young wife who doesn't altogether trust David to shun temptation without a helping hand. But even the most trying circumstances can't quench her natural gaiety for long and she should be allowed the occasional glimpse of skittishness, especially when things begin to go her way.

The actress playing Maria clearly needs looks and a good figure but above all she must bring to the play that touch of Mediterranean colour and temperament which throws David's quiet little world topsy-turvy. This can be assisted by her wardrobe, which should be as luscious and spectacular as possible. Beware of making Maria too hard and heartless. Admittedly she makes the most of her unfair feminine advantages over David but she does it so nicely that the male section of the audience at least should be left with the impression that, in spite of her parentage, she's a nice girl at heart. Her scenes with Cellini should be played dramatically to give substance to the underlying plot.

Mrs. Scott is a complex character. On the surface feather-brained and giddy she has, in fact, a commanding personality and is a born organizer, whether of old people's outings, picnics or truculent landladies. Much of the fun should stem from her unruffled acceptance of the most extraordinary situations which she swiftly turns to her own advantage. The actress playing the part should give the impression of upper-middle class well-being and should aim to strike a happy medium between appearing too vague or too domineering.

The Taxi Driver/Burglar is a cheerful Cockney who has taken to crime to supplement his income. Although he takes himself and his professional activities very seriously, this is a broad comedy part and should be played for laughs throughout. To give point to his various transformations he must, of course, be immediately recognizable to the audience beneath his "disguises", perhaps by adopting a characteristic trick of style such as a distinctive walk.

Mrs. Bottle, too, is a broad comedy part and can be played almost as a caricature.

Mrs. MacWhimble should preferably be physically and vocally powerful and domineering. Grudging and suspicious after a life-time's experience of undesirable tenants, she has the disposition of sour wine. The audience should be made to feel that the late Mr. MacWhimble is better off wherever he is. Only when she crosses swords with Mrs. Scott in Act Two does she meet her match. Stripped of her truculence she is a poor thing.

Cellini: good strong melodramatic stuff here—sword-stick and all—with a general air of villainy and twirling moustachios. There should be a striking contrast between his oily charm with Mrs. Scott and his bullying attitude towards Maria. A thoroughly unpleasant character who deserves all he gets.

The Curate, poor soul, is mild and unworldly and inevitably destined for disaster. He probably came into the world wearing pince-nez and with an indestructible faith in the milk of human kindness which even exploding geysers cannot entirely destroy.

One or two general points on staging. The play lends itself readily to a simple lighting plot and a basic set. Some producers may, however, prefer something more adventurous and the original Erith production adopted a cutaway effect on Stage Right with back projection and cloud effects suggesting the roof-top view outside by day and by night. Care should be taken to avoid making the set too dismal. Lighting must be good even during the late night scene or part of the action will be lost. Adequate lighting will also help to counter the depressive effect of the more ancient articles of furniture. Kate, too, has done her best in difficult circumstances and her influence is shown in the gaiety of the curtains, cushion covers, etc., which all help to brighten the place up. The general impression should be of two young people, recently married, making a pretty good stab at a tolerable standard of living on rather slender means.

J.A.D.

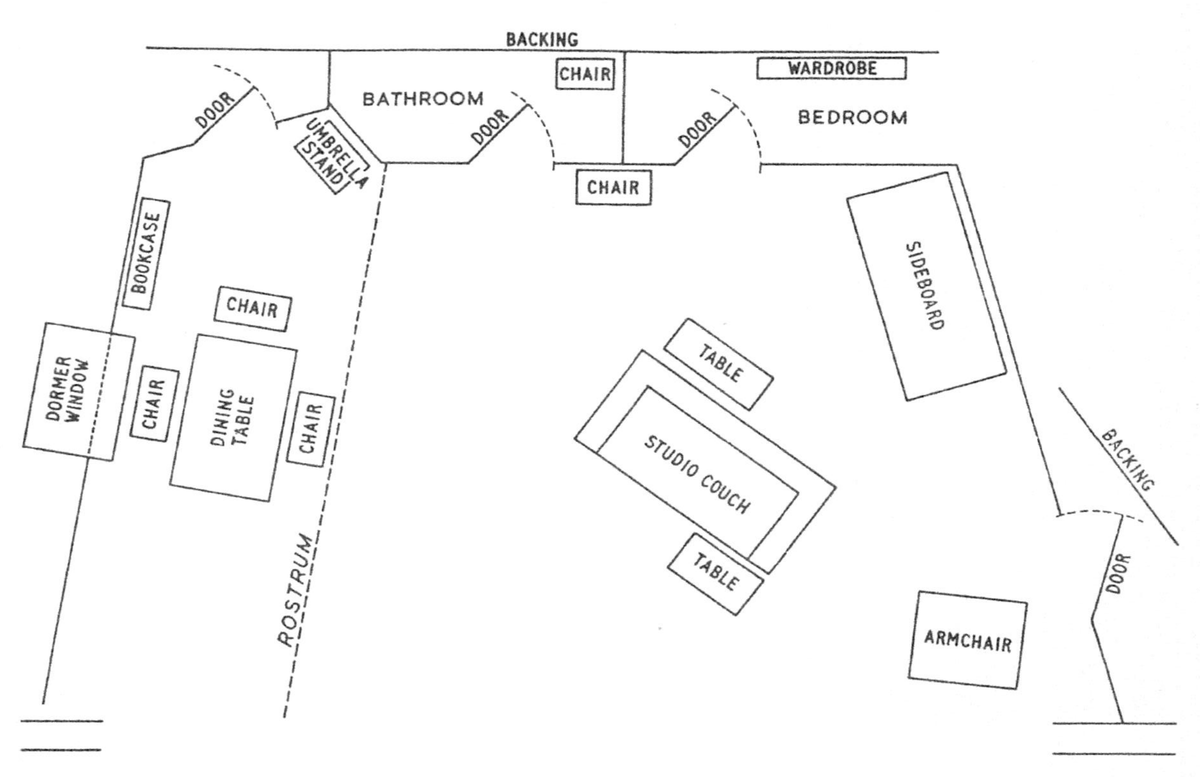

BACKING
CHAIR
WARDROBE
BATHROOM
DOOR
DOOR
BEDROOM
DOOR
UMBRELLA STAND
CHAIR
SIDEBOARD
BOOKCASE
CHAIR
TABLE
BACKING
DORMER WINDOW
CHAIR
DINING TABLE
CHAIR
STUDIO COUCH
ROSTRUM
TABLE
DOOR
ARMCHAIR

CAT ON THE FIDDLE

ACT ONE

SCENE I

The action of the play takes place in the living-room of a small and thoroughly inconvenient second-floor flat in London.

It is an unattractive room and the general effect is not improved by the addition of one or two items of contemporary furnishing, notably a studio couch, among the older inhabitants which are predominantly of 1920 vintage.

A door D.L. leads to the kitchen. C.B. are two other doors. The one on the R. is conspicuously and incongruously marked "Bathroom", the second leads into the bedroom. The main entrance to the flat is at a slightly higher level and set at an angle U.R. The whole right-hand side of the room is at this slightly higher level, suggesting that it was once two smaller rooms converted into one. This effect is further emphasized by the dormer window and sloping ceiling R.

The studio couch stands obliquely L.C., and below it is a small coffee-table with a portable record player. Behind the couch another and higher table carrying a table-lamp and telephone. U.L. an ornate sideboard with a suspicious number of bottles and glasses and a transistor radio. L. of the main entrance an umbrella-stand with a solitary umbrella and on the dais, under the window, a frail-looking dining-table with the remains of a meal. Old-fashioned dining-chairs to match, one of which stands against the wall between the bedroom and bathroom doors. Above the table a small book-case well stuffed with papers, knitting, etc. Below the kitchen door an easy chair with startling upholstery. A scattering of cushions and L.P. record jackets lends a touch of colour to the room and various papers and magazines lying around on the floor and furniture give it a "well-lived in" air. On the back wall hang two unglazed pictures. The one nearer the front door is extremely modern and completely incomprehensible; the other is a reproduction of "Dante and Beatrice" and well faded at that. On the L. wall the "Monarch of the Glen"

On a nail in the bathroom door hangs a large printed notice—"Engaged".

As the curtain rises DAVID, a personable fellow of 28, is sitting on the couch, book in hand, listening to an Italian Linguaphone record and repeating phrases in a faltering voice and a horrible accent. He is in shirt-sleeves without collar or tie. The voice on the record is female.

After a few moments of this KATE, *his wife, enters. She is 24, pretty, with a snub nose and a determined chin. At present she is clearly bent on business. An apron covers a smart suit and her whole appearance suggests a last-minute rush before going away. Ignoring* DAVID, *she crosses to* C., *switches on a vacuum cleaner which stands centre stage plugged into the standard lamp and attacks the crumbs under the table. The cleaner is a horror of a thing, old and deafening.* DAVID *closes his book with a gesture of despair and turns off the record player. He stands and shouts something, but the cleaner drowns his words.* KATE *continues to clean ferociously.* DAVID *comes into her line of vision and waves his arms about vigorously mouthing words.* KATE *switches off.*

KATE. Cold?

DAVID. Must you make that unearthly row?

KATE. Yes. (*She stoops to switch on again.*)

DAVID. But I can't hear what I'm saying.

KATE. Neither can I. (*She switches on.*)

(DAVID *waits until the work is well under way again and* KATE'S *back turned, then quickly switches off again at the table-lamp. He leans back on the couch and awaits results.* KATE *regards the nozzle of her expiring cleaner in some surprise.*)

Damn! (*She gives the cleaner a hearty kick.*) Work, you decrepit old wind-bag! David, it's no good, you'll have to buy me a new one.

DAVID (*looking up innocently from his book*). What's that? Oh, have you finished?

KATE (*crossly*). Does it look as though I have?

DAVID (*gazing vacantly round the room*). Yes. Jolly nice. Now I'll just— (*He moves towards the record player.*)

KATE. Oh no, you don't. (*She advances to* C., *pointing the nozzle of the cleaner at him accusingly.*) Just you lend a hand, my lad; sitting there like an advert for Turkish Delight!

DAVID. Now, now, don't insult the sultan. (*He assumes a cross-legged attitude on the couch and claps his hands.*) Bring on my favourite dancing-girl.

(KATE *reaches into her apron pocket and throws a duster into his hands.*)

KATE. Here you are, you wicked old potentate. Full of Eastern promise. Warm from my bare pocket. Now get cracking.

(*During the ensuing dialogue they move round the room dusting, although* DAVID'S *contribution is not particularly useful, as he is still holding his book in one hand and invariably chooses to dust the articles* KATE *has just finished.*)

DAVID. I thought you cleaned this room last week.

KATE. Honestly, David, I do believe you'd live in a pig-sty if I let you.

DAVID (*grunting*). Am I boring you? (*He nuzzles her neck.*)

KATE. That'll do. Dust!

DAVID. Oh Lord, this is supposed to be my holiday. Don't you think we've done enough? (*He collapses on the step.*)

KATE. What time is it?

DAVID (*consulting his watch*). Let's see. This says a quarter to four—that makes it about two-thirty.

KATE. Why on earth don't you keep it right?

DAVID. Well, I did put it right last Tuesday, but it gains a bit.

KATE. It's certainly got more energy than you. (*She pushes the cleaner close to the couch and crosses to the bathroom, taking off her apron.*) I shall have to leave the rest to you. Do try to make it look presentable before he arrives. (*She goes into bathroom.*)

DAVID (*who has returned to his book and is dusting with one hand while reading*). Right-ho! (*Looking up.*) Who?

KATE (*looking out of the bathroom with powder and puff and dabbing at her nose*). Your guest, dear. The wonderful Señor Lauro or whatever his name is.

DAVID. Oh, Mario, you mean. He won't mind roughing it a bit. And Kate dear, it's Signore—remember? Italian. S—I—G—N—

KATE. Oh!

DAVID. That's right. —R—E.

KATE. I don't care if he's a Japanese mandarin with long pigtail moustaches! I still think the whole thing's crazy. (*And having spoken she disappears into the bedroom.*)

DAVID (*considering this possibility*). There wouldn't be much point in me learning Italian if he can only talk Japaneesy. Anyway, I don't think mandarins come from Japan. They're a sort of orange. I'll look it up. (*He moves towards the book-case, but KATE reappears.*)

KATE. Don't you dare. You can keep your old books for Signor Lauro.

DAVID. Are you sure you won't stay and meet him?

KATE. No, thank you. It's been bad enough you asking for your breakfast in Italian. I couldn't stand two of you at it. (*She crosses to the bathroom.*) I wouldn't mind so much if I knew what you were on about; but I can't help feeling you're being rude behind my back— so I do. (*She disappears into the bathroom.*)

DAVID. Do what?

KATE (*her head appearing again*). Mind!

DAVID. Oh!

KATE. Now do go and put on a tie, David. Mother will be here with the car any minute.

    (*Her head disappears again. DAVID, immersed in his book, crosses to the couch, reaches out for his tie, which is over the back of the couch, and starts to put it on without bothering about the collar. KATE, now dressed for going out, emerges finally from the bathroom.*)

I can't think why I agreed to the crazy idea in the first place. (*She observes his activities.*) David! (*She leads him by the tie to the bathroom.*) Collar and tie. And hurry up!

 (*She goes into the kitchen. There is a knock at the door and the nearest picture falls off its hook.*)

(*Off.*) Answer the door, there's a sweet. It's Mother, I expect.

 (DAVID *re-enters, book in one hand, collar and tie in the other, a sports jacket slung over one arm. He opens the door.*)

DAVID (*without looking*). Hello, Mother-in-law.

 (*Enter* MRS. MACWHIMBLE. *She is clearly not* KATE'S *mother, being wrapped in a voluminous overall. Her arms are red, muscular and folded; her face grim; her hair drawn back into a severe and uncompromising bun. She is, in fact,* DAVID'S *landlady from the flat below. Thus addressed she gives him a cold, hard glare.*)

Oh! My mistake—thank goodness.

KATE (*off*). Is that you, Mummy?

DAVID (*calling*). No, dear, it's Mrs. MacRumble—MacWhimble I mean. (*He replaces the picture.*)

KATE. Oh! (*She enters, wiping her hands.*) Good afternoon, Mrs. MacWhimble. What a nice surprise. (*She moves to* C.)

DAVID (*registering extreme horror*). Lovely! The rent must be due. (*He gets another glare from the visitor.*)

MRS. MAC (*ignoring* DAVID *and addressing* KATE). You're going away I believe. (*It is more of an accusation than a question.*)

KATE. Why, yes. Mummy's taking me round to look after granny for a few days.

DAVID. She's expecting.

MRS. MAC. Expecting!

DAVID. Yes. She's been like it for years. Always expecting Kate to go and look after her.

KATE. Shut up, David.

MRS. MAC. Women's place is in the 'ome.

DAVID (*crossing to couch and depositing his coat, collar and tie*). That's what granny always says—her home.

KATE. Is anything wrong, Mrs. MacWhimble?

MRS. MAC (*coming closer to* KATE *and addressing her in a sinister whisper*). I come to warn you!

KATE. Warn me?

MRS. MAC (*jerking her thumb at* DAVID). About 'im. 'E ain't safe—not on 'is own. They never are. Hmph! Men! I knows 'em.

DAVID. You wicked old rascal!

MRS. MAC (*steadfastly ignoring him*). 'Elpless as new-born 'ippopotamuses, they are. Leave 'em alone for five minutes and they're in a fine pickle.

DAVID. I didn't know 'ippopotamuses liked pickle.

KATE. But David will be all right on his own. He's very capable.

MRS. MAC. Capable of anything I'd say. (*She lowers her voice.*) It ain't 'is being alone what worries me.

DAVID (*jumping up and coming forward*). Oh, if it's Mario you're thinking about— Ow!

   (KATE *has kicked his shin and he retires to the couch hurt.*)

MRS. MAC. 'Oo?

KATE. That's what we call the cat.

MRS. MAC. I didn't know you 'ad a cat.

KATE. You may not have noticed him—he's very thin. By the way, did you know we get smoke coming out from under the bath?

MRS. MAC. Wot?

KATE. You really ought to send for a plumber at once.

DAVID (*holding his shin*). Or a doctor.

MRS. MAC (*draws from her apron pocket a well-thumbed copy of the lease and reads from it*). 'Ere, wait a minute. "Tenants is responsible for all repairs and replacements to furniture and fittings"—and baths is fittings.

DAVID. That one's a very tight fitting.

MRS. MAC (*making for the door*). I'll call the plumber at once—and tell 'im to send you the bill.

KATE (*shepherding her out*). Thank you, Mrs. MacWhimble.

DAVID. And may your aspidistras never get the green-fly.

MRS. MAC (*wagging her finger at him*). And just you remember, any trouble from you while Mrs. Abbott's away and I'll cut off yer 'ot water.

   (*She goes out, banging the door. The picture falls off the wall and* KATE *replaces it.*)

DAVID. Exit the wicked fairy in a shower of hairpins. (*He inspects his outraged shin.*) What's the idea of crippling me? (*He hobbles over and takes from the book-case a sheet of cardboard, a crayon and an india-rubber. He sits on the couch with his feet up, facing the bathroom, and sets to work.*)

KATE. Oh, you know what she's like about visitors. Seems to think their one ambition is to stop up the sink or leave ball-bearings on the stairs. Now get dressed before mother arrives, there's a dear. She ought to be here by now. (*She goes into the bedroom.*)

DAVID. There's a little job I want to finish first.

KATE (*off*). Does Mario like animals?

DAVID. He said in his last letter that he loved baby sheep roasted.

KATE (*looking in*). Can he handle baby 'ippopotamuses?

   (DAVID *throws the rubber at her. There is a knock on the door and the picture falls.*)

I'll get it.

(*She restores the picture and opens the door. Enter* MRS. SCOTT, KATE'S *mother. She is middle-aged, extremely smart and bustling, with the occasional hint of vagueness. A very strong character.*)

Hello, Mummy darling.

(*They kiss.*)

I'm nearly ready. (*She goes into the bedroom.*)

MRS. SCOTT. Hello, dear. Hello, David, how are you? (DAVID *grunts and waves a hand.*) I'm a wee bit late, I'm afraid, but I had trouble with the car. I think the man said my plackets were loose, but that doesn't sound quite right. (*She sits in easy chair* D.L.)

DAVID. Gaskets.

MRS. SCOTT. What an expressive word. I must remember it next time I play bridge. What are you doing, David?

(DAVID *rises and holds up his cardboard against the bathroom door.*)

DAVID. There, that should do the trick. No more accidents, eh?

(*It reads "Out of Order. Please use the Bell". As he is holding it it appears to refer to the bathroom.* MRS. SCOTT *crosses and looks hard at the title on the door.*)

MRS. SCOTT. How very inconvenient. Is it a big bell?

DAVID. No, no, you don't understand. I'm going to hang this on the knocker. (*He crosses to the sideboard.*)

MRS. SCOTT. But the knocker isn't out of order.

(*Enter* KATE *from the bedroom. She is carrying a small suitcase which she puts down by the bedroom door.*)

KATE. Here we are then. What's that? (*She reads the placard over* DAVID'S *shoulder.*) But it isn't out of order.

DAVID (*a little peevishly*). I know that. But we've got to consider Psyche. Where's the hammer? (*He rummages about in the sideboard and emerges with a very small tack hammer and a tin of tacks.*)

MRS. SCOTT. Who's Psyche?

DAVID. That is. (*He points at the picture.*) Poor girl's bruised all over. (*He pats the picture-frame affectionately and goes outside to fix the notice.*)

KATE (*looking after him doubtfully*). I suppose it's safe to leave him?

MRS. SCOTT (*sitting again in the easy chair*). Of course. I left your father dozens of times. It did him the world of good.

KATE. Yes, but that wasn't quite the same.

MRS. SCOTT. Besides, hasn't he got a friend coming to keep him company?

KATE. That's what's worrying me. You see, we don't really know much about this friend of his. (*She sits on couch.*)

MRS. SCOTT. But surely David must know him quite well or he wouldn't have invited him.

(*There is a prolonged hammering from outside and the picture falls.*)

KATE. You don't know David. Remember last time you were here he was taking a course in pottery?

MRS. SCOTT. Yes. He made me such a charming ash-tray, I remember.

KATE. It was supposed to be a jug. Well, now it's Italian. (*More hammering.*)

MRS. SCOTT. Italian pottery?

KATE. No—language.

MRS. SCOTT. Oh, what a pity. I saw a delightful little Italian vase in that antique shop round the corner and I wanted an expert opinion.

KATE. Not quite in David's line, I'm afraid. He doesn't know a spade from a Spode.

(*Hammering.*)

MRS. SCOTT. Dear boy. What is he doing out there?

KATE. Putting in a drawing pin, I expect.

MRS. SCOTT. And I suppose he met this—what's his name?

KATE. Mario Lauro.

MRS. SCOTT. Such lovely names they have. Well, I suppose he met him at evening classes.

KATE. No such luck. He's never set eyes on him.

(*Devastating hammering.*)

(*Shouting.*) David! For goodness' sake.

(*More hammering.* KATE *crosses to the door and calls maliciously.*) You see, Mummy, Mario is David's "pen pal". (*The hammering stops at once and* DAVID *enters brandishing the tack hammer.*)

DAVID. Italian correspondent, if you don't mind.

(*He gives the picture hook a bang or two for good measure, then rehangs the picture.*)

KATE. They've been writing incomprehensible letters to one another for about three months.

MRS. SCOTT. Well, I wouldn't worry, dear, if I were you. I'm sure David's well able to look after himself.

DAVID (*bowing*). Thank you, Mother-in-law. Efficiency incorporated. (*He shuts the door reasonably gently and the picture falls off the hook.*) Gaskets! (*He replaces the picture yet again.*)

MRS. SCOTT (*rising and pulling herself together*). Well, dear, if you're not going to offer me a drink, we might as well get started.

DAVID. Sorry. Not a very good host. Will you have home-made ginger beer or some of Great-aunt Mabel's rhubarb and dandelion?

MRS. SCOTT. On second thoughts, perhaps I won't risk it. The police would never believe me. Ready, Catherine?

(KATE *pats her hair into place, looking into the mirror which hangs on the "fourth wall".*)

DAVID. Sure you won't wait and meet Mario? His train is due in about an hour.

MRS. SCOTT. We really shouldn't. I want to be home before seven. The car does the most extraordinary things after dark. It leaps at unsuspecting old men and stops at lamp-posts.

KATE. But, Mummy dear, it isn't all that far.

MRS. SCOTT. You never know. I spent an hour and a half once trying to find my way out of Regent's Park Zoo. (*She crosses to front door.*)

DAVID. But you're not supposed to take cars into the zoo.

MRS. SCOTT. Yes, I know, dear. That's what made it all so difficult.

(KATE *picks up her suitcase.*)

KATE. Good-bye then, darling.

DAVID. Good-bye, my sweet.

KATE. Take care.

(*They kiss.*)

There's lots of food in the larder and I've told the milkman to leave an extra pint in case of emergencies.

DAVID. Right-ho!

KATE. The butcher closes at three on Wednesdays and don't forget to switch the water on before you light the gas in the geyser.

DAVID. Yes, yes. Right-ho!

KATE. And you know where the first-aid box is.

MRS. SCOTT. Really, Catherine, anyone would think David was as helpless as a new-born—

KATE. 'Ippopotamus. He is, the darling. Good-bye.

DAVID. Cheerio, darling. Good-bye.

(*He sees them out of the door, then returns to the couch with his book and flops down. Re-enter* KATE.)

KATE. Good-bye darling. Be careful won't you and—(*She rushes over and kisses him tearfully.*) put your collar and tie on before Mario arrives.

(*She runs off, banging the door.* DAVID *rushes over to catch the picture which stays put. He turns round with a smirk of triumph rubbing his hands as at a good job done. The telephone rings and the picture falls.*)

DAVID (*into the phone*). Hello?—Yes, Mr. Abbott speaking—Who?— Oh, the plumber.—Hmmm?—Well, it's the bathroom—no, not a leak, we get smoke coming out from underneath.—What?—No it's not the flue, it's the bath.—Oh, you have the flu. Bad luck. Draughty pipes, I expect.—Yes, of course—your mate—old what?—your old Chinaman?—Oh, never mind. You will?—Jolly good—tomorrow then. Oh, I say, you don't happen to be a picture hanger as well, I suppose?—Not? Pity. No, it doesn't matter. We'll expect your old Chinese mate tomorrow then. Yes—Good-bye. (*He hangs up.*) Chinese plumbers? (*He puts on his collar and tie in front of the mirror, addressing his reflection.*) Me Peeping Tom. You got leakee? Old Chinese Ploverb him say "Honolable gentleman velly unhappy, him spling leak in illustlious tappee." (*He puts on his jacket.*) Now then. Tidy up.

(*His method of tidying is a model of male efficiency. He gathers up an armful of papers and magazines and decants them behind the sofa, at the same time steering the cleaner out of sight with his foot. He gathers the four corners of the tablecloth together, thus making a clean sweep of the remnants of lunch. He almost throws this into the kitchen, but changes his mind at the last minute and swings round once or twice with it while it loses momentum, then carries it out into the kitchen gently. Cushions fly. The gramophone lid goes down with a bang. Crumbs are brushed under a rug with* KATE's *best table runner, which is then deftly flicked across the table. An empty wine-bottle is snatched from the bookcase and plonked on to the table and two knitting-needles with knitting attached are pushed into the neck of the bottle, where they hang like some exotic flower. He marches to the door, then pauses and surveys the result of his labours with a self-satisfied smile. The whole job has taken little more than a minute.*)

I really don't know what they find to do all day! (*He replaces the picture and consults his watch.*) Twenty minutes to the station. Mustn't be late or he'll get lost. Heigh-ho!

He goes out singing "A Bachelor Gay" and crashes the door behind him. The singing stops and a moment later his head reappears. He regards the unmoved picture with satisfaction and gives it a conspiratorial nod. He closes the door very, very gently. The picture falls and so does the CURTAIN

SCENE 2

Later the same day. It is growing dark. The picture still lies where it fell at the end of Scene 1.

The door-bell rings insistently. After a pause the knocker is heard, then the bell again. After a further interval the door is opened gingerly and a head appears wearing a peaked cap. Enter a taxi-driver, a small, shifty-looking man.

TAXIMAN. Anyone about? (*Nothing happens.*) Ship ahoy! Anybody in? Let's 'ave a bit of light on the scene. (*He switches on the light by the door and walks in whistling. He carries a very large suitcase. Suddenly he sees the "Engaged" notice on the bathroom door and stops short.*) Oh! The island's in'abited. (*He leaves the case in the middle of the floor and goes to the bathroom door, where he makes coughing noises.*) 'Allo? (*He knocks politely at the empty room—nothing happens.*) Cor lummee!

Must be asleep in the bath. (*He raises his voice.*) 'Allo there! Any-one at 'ome?

(*Enter* MARIA. *She is dark and exotic and her figure breath-taking. Expensively and flamboyantly dressed, she moves with a natural and unselfconscious voluptuousness which cannot fail to turn a man's head in more ways than one. Her English is good, with sufficient accent to give charm to her simplest remark.*)

(*A little unsteadily in view of her closeness.*) Oh! 'Allo, miss. Made me jump. Seems there ain't nobody at 'ome. Or else (*He points to the bathroom.*)—one of the old ladies 'as been took bad.

MARIA. Old ladies? There are old ladies 'ere?

TAXIMAN. Figure of speech, miss. You know, old ladies locked in the —er—bathroom.

MARIA (*coming further into the room and looking around*). I suppose this is the right 'ouse. Is very small.

TAXIMAN (*coming forward*). This is it all right, miss. Number 187a. Small but cosy.

MARIA. They are not 'aving much money?

TAXIMAN. You can't always go by the looks of things. You'd be surprised at some of the things I've picked up—er—seen in 'ouses like this. 'Aven't got a telly either—that's a good sign. I'll go and get the rest of your stuff.

(*He goes out.* MARIA *inspects the room, replaces the picture and then pokes her head into the bedroom. The* TAXIMAN *returns, struggling with another enormous case.*)

'Ere we are then, miss. (*He puts it down beside the other.*) Good job you're travelling light.

MARIA. I think I like it 'ere. Is different.

(*She examines the unusual table decorations with interest.*)

TAXIMAN. Funny there ain't nobody in, though. Unless they're sitting tight in the bath. (*He goes to the bathroom door and knocks loudly.*) Anybody there? Speak now or for ever 'old your peace. I'm a-coming in. (*He looks in and turns on the light.*) Only an old bath-towel and a bit of soap. I suppose they knew you was coming?

MARIA. Oh, yes.

TAXIMAN. I'd 'ave took good care to be 'ere waiting if it was me.

MARIA. If what was you?

TAXIMAN. If 'e was me.

MARIA. 'Oo?

TAXIMAN. The bloke waiting 'ere for you.

MARIA. But there is no one.

TAXIMAN (*taking off his cap and scratching his head*). I've sort of lost track of this conversation.

MARIA. Never mind. Perhaps you are being a nice kind man and taking the cases into the bedroom. Is over there.

TAXIMAN. You 'aven't wasted much time. (*He starts to hump the cases into the bedroom.*) Of course, you know, I'm not really supposed to do this sort of thing. It upsets me union.

MARIA. You 'ave a union?

TAXIMAN. Yus, of course I 'ave.

MARIA. It is troublesome?

TAXIMAN. Oh, the usual sort of thing.

MARIA. Is unpleasant when it starts shooting.

TAXIMAN. Lumme! We 'aven't got to that state—not yet.

MARIA (*crossing to couch*). But you must take care. My mother, she 'ave a union once and could not wear 'er shoe for a week. (*She sits, takes off her shoe and caresses a shapely foot.*)

TAXIMAN. You know, miss, I don't think you and me are talking about the same sort of union. Mine's a big gathering of chaps—

MARIA. It is the same thing exactly. Very big and swollen and full of anguish.

TAXIMAN. Maybe you're right. Well, that's done. I must be off or I'll miss me Rosie Lee.

MARIA. Ah! She is your girl?

TAXIMAN. Bless yer 'eart. I got a missus and four kids.

MARIA. And your wife, she is knowing about this Rosie?

TAXIMAN. Come off it. Rosie Lee, you know—me char.

MARIA. Is 'ard work for a young girl.

TAXIMAN. Gawd love old Ireland, you ain't safe let loose. You don't understand plain English.

MARIA. Is no matter. How much am I owing you? (*She seizes her handbag and takes out a handful of notes which she thrusts at him.*)

TAXIMAN. Now you're talking. (*He notices the money.*) Cor blimey, mate, you giving it away?

MARIA. You take what it is I am owing you. I do not follow this money.

    (*He takes a ten-shilling note and fishes in his pocket for change.*)

TAXIMAN. I'd follow money anywhere. 'Ere y'are, miss. 'Arf a dollar change. (*He goes to the door.*) Be all right on your Jack Jones? By yourself, I mean.

MARIA (*putting the notes on the coffee-table*). But of course.

TAXIMAN (*eyeing the money*). I wouldn't leave that lot lying around if I was you. There's a lot of bad characters about. 'Ow much is there?

MARIA (*stuffing it into her handbag*). I dunno. 'Undred pound, I think. I am only on a leetle 'oliday.

TAXIMAN (*licking his lips*). A 'undred nicker! Just asking to be picked up. Good job I'm honest. Well, be seeing you. (*He goes out.*)

MARIA (*calling after him*). *Arrivederci* and try a mustard plaster on your union. (*Alone, she reclines on the couch, takes a note-book and package from her hand-bag and, having located the phone, dials 100.*) 'Allo?—Operator. Please to give me (*She consults a note-book.*) — 'OP 3342—*Che?*—'OP—Haitch Ho Pee—Is what I say, 'OP—*si.* (*A pause.*) 'Allo? (*She speaks conspiratorially.*) Cellini?—Maria, *si.* I am 'ere—Of course I 'ave it—*Si*, yes, tonight—all right, you will collect it then? When?—two o'clock! What in the morning?—*Si, si*, is dangerous—all right, all right, I leave the door open. Two o'clock, *bene.* (*She puts the phone down.*) *Madre mia!* (*She picks up the phone again and dials 100.*) 'Allo, 'allo—Operator? I wish to make a call to Naples—*Si*, yes, Naples—is in Italy, yes—*grazie.* (*She waits a moment.*) 'Allo?—I want Napoli 87053—Signore Carlo Pasqualini—A personal call? Yes, is very personal, you must not listen in. My number? (*She consults the dial.*) Is Wild Green 5892—Signorina Lauro—You will ring back? *Grazie*—Good-bye.

> (*She puts the phone down, pats the little package and returns it into the depths of her handbag. She then goes into the bedroom and turns on the light. As the bedroom door closes behind her the front door opens and* DAVID *enters. He takes off his jacket and throws it over a chair, pats the picture affectionately and then notices the light is on. He shrugs.*)

DAVID. Must have left it on. Now then—(*He rubs his hands and stands* c. *for a moment, at a loss.*) Cup of tea—that's it. Where's the jolly old kettle. (*He disappears into the kitchen.* MARIA *emerges from the bedroom carrying a bath-robe, towel and washing-bag and enters the bathroom, closing the door.* DAVID *reappears, picks up his book and throws himself on to the couch.*) I don't know. (*He yawns.*) Fancy him missing the train—he must be a bit of a fathead.

> (*There is a noise from the bathroom and his ears prick up. He listens for a moment, but all is quiet and he returns to his book. He yawns again, stretches and throws the book aside.*)

Well, this won't do. (*He leaps to his feet.*) I think I'll have a bath.

> (*He starts to take off his collar and tie, walks towards the radio which stands on the sideboard and is about to switch it on when the sound of singing comes from the bathroom. He stops dead with his hand stretched out towards the radio.*)

Good Lord! (*He puts his hand down and the singing stops.*) The damned thing's bewitched!

> (*The singing starts again and he suddenly realizes it is coming from the bathroom.*)

Katie! (*He stalks over and opens the bathroom door.*) Katie, what on earth are you do— (*He whips smartly out again and slams the door, standing pale and anguished with his back to it.*) My God, wrong house! (*He makes for the front door, then stops and considers.*) No. Right house, wrong body. Burglars! (*There are noises from the bathroom and he runs over and seizes the phone. As he dials 999 he calls out nervously.*) D-don't move, you're uncovered. I mean I've got you covered. (*Into phone.*) Hello, hello? Yes, emergency! Police, quick! (*Shouting towards the bathroom.*) S-stay where you are—the door's locked. (*Into phone.*) Hello, police? I want to report a— (MARIA *comes out of the bathroom in her bath-robe. She looks ravishing.*) a beautiful girl in my bathroom. (*The telephone comes away from his ear and he tucks it into his trouser pocket.*)

MARIA. 'Allo.

DAVID (*weakly*). Hello! (*The phone gibbers and squeaks. He looks all round for it and puts it back to his ear.*) Hello?—Description? Oh, about five foot four. Dark hair. Lovely brown eyes, delicious lips and—what?—Just a bath-robe! Hmmm? Oh. (*To* MARIA.) Any distinguishing marks?

MARIA (*pointing to her left buttock*). A mole.

DAVID (*into phone*). A mole on her left—er—cheek.—You what? You'll come round the minute you're off duty? Good show. (*He puts the phone down without taking his eyes off* MARIA, *who comes forward to shake hands.*)

MARIA. 'Allo, David.

DAVID (*shaking hands like a man in a dream*). How do you do. Er—who?

MARIA. You were not expecting me so soon?

DAVID (*edging away to the far side of the couch*). Not exactly. Er—Kate is out. Perhaps if you tried next week.

MARIA. Ah, David, you make the fun. Of course Kate is out. You say so in your letter.

DAVID (*aghast*). My letter!

MARIA. Of course. I am Maria. You are dissipated?

DAVID. No, I don't think so—at least—I, I— Good Lord! (*He totters to the easy-chair and sits down.*)

MARIA (*moving towards him*). You are ill?

DAVID. No, no. Just a bit—overwhelmed. I seem to have got my genders in a tangle!

MARIA. Ah! Your letters, they were very funny. All mixed up. You are a crazy mixed up kid, eh?

DAVID (*vaguely*). 'Ippopotamus.

MARIA (*perching on the arm of the chair and showing a good deal of leg*). Well, I am 'ere all the same.

DAVID (*jumping up anxiously*). I say, don't you think you ought to put something else on? It's a bit chilly.

MARIA. But I am comfortable this way. You don't like it?

DAVID. Yes—I mean no—I mean—well, it's all so dashed unexpected.

MARIA (*pouting*). Ah, you are un'appy with me.

DAVID. No, rather not! It's just that—well—you're not quite what I was expecting. Have you got a brother?

MARIA. No. A little sister. Is very lonely.

DAVID. Oh, I say, bad luck.

MARIA (*sadly*). And now you don't like me. I go away. (*She makes a move towards the door.*)

DAVID. Oh, I say, don't do that. I mean you can't go out like that. Have a—have a drink or something. (*He pours himself a large rhubarb and dandelion.*)

MARIA (*subsiding on to the couch*). Is better. A big one, please.

(DAVID *swallows his drink at a gulp, pulls a face and pours two more.*)

DAVID. Don't mind me. Just a slight case of shock. I'm not really used to finding strange women in the bathroom and (*He looks at her reclining voluptuously on the couch.*)—and—er—all that sort of thing.

MARIA. Poor David. (*He hands her a drink and she pats the couch invitingly.*) Come 'ere and tell me all about it. (*He sits gingerly on the edge of the couch.*)

DAVID. All about what?

MARIA. All about whatever it is that you are un'appy about.

DAVID. Well—

(MARIA *raises her glass and holds him with her eyes across the brim, then she sips.*)

MARIA. Is nice.

DAVID. I say, do you like it? It's a very old remedy—er—recipe of my Great-aunt Mabel's. (*He sips and pulls a wry face.*) She's a witch. Lives in a house with a hundred cats and an old gander called Jane.

MARIA. Is a funny name for a gander.

DAVID. Yes, but you see they christened it before they found out and didn't like to hurt its feelings afterwards. (*He is now more at his ease and is sitting on the couch almost nonchalantly.*)

MARIA. Poor old goosey-gander. 'Ow can anyone make a mistake like that?

DAVID (*groaning*). Oh, Lord! I say, Signorina—

MARIA. It was "Maria" in your letters.

DAVID. Oh, was it? Katie always said my handwriting was shocking. Well, Maria, then—

MARIA (*huskily*). Is better. I like to 'ear you say my name, David.

DAVID (*sitting up very straight and looking in front of him*). I'm sorry about all this. I mean—well—nobody here when you arrived.

MARIA. Is no worry. I am 'ere.

DAVID. Yes, that's just the trouble.

MARIA. David!

DAVID. Oh, what the hell! Have some more of Auntie's special. (*He jumps up and goes to the sideboard.*)

MARIA. *Momento.* I bring something for you. (*She goes into the bedroom.*) (*Off.*) I am telling the customs man it is cough mixture. (*She brings in a bottle of brandy.*)

DAVID (*who has seized the opportunity to mop his brow*). I say! You know, Maria, you're a bit of a lass. (*He opens the bottle and pours.*)

MARIA. I am all of a lass. (*She pirouettes in front of him.*) Each part, you see.

DAVID. By George! (*He gulps down his glass of brandy and refills.*)

MARIA (*holding up her glass*). To a 'appy 'oliday, David.

DAVID (*heavily*). 'Appy 'oliday. (*He drinks.*)

MARIA (*meaningly*). Together! (*She drinks while* DAVID *splutters, then she curls up on the couch.*) Is cosy. Is nice being intimate on the sofa. I am so glad you ask me to come, David.

DAVID. Did I? Oh yes—so am I, I think. (*The brandy is beginning to work and he joins her on the couch, taking the bottle with him.*)

MARIA. Kate did not mind?

DAVID. N-no. I hope not.

MARIA. Sisterly understanding, eh?

DAVID. Sisterly!

MARIA. She trusts 'er big brother, is nice. (*She puts her head on his shoulder.*)

DAVID. Is awful! My Italian must be worse than I thought. I'll burn that bloody dictionary! (*He refills his glass and as an afterthought fills* MARIA's.)

MARIA (*looking round*). Is a nice 'ouse.

DAVID (*nodding glumly*). Yes, is.

MARIA. Just room for two.

DAVID. Yes, well, I was just thinking you might like a bit of company. (*He tries to get up, but she holds him.*)

MARIA. Oh, don't go.

DAVID. I was just going to phone old Auntie and ask her round for a week or two. She gets awfully lonely all by herself with a hundred cats.

MARIA. And the goosey-gander. David, you are afraid of me!

DAVID. Good Lord, yes—I mean no!

MARIA (*snuggling up*). But you invite me to come.

DAVID. It was a mistake.

MARIA (*taking his hand and stroking it*). Was it?

DAVID (*almost succumbs, but recovers just in time*). Here, let me show you round the house. (*He jumps up.*)

MARIA. But I have seen him.

DAVID (*running round like mad, brandishing the bottle*). No, you can't have—not all of him. Look here—bathroom, see, hot and cold running all over the place. The other performance is out there through the kitchen. Well-appointed front door knocker and every-thing, and—er—bedroom. (MARIA *sits watching him half-amused as he leans panting against the bedroom door.*)

MARIA. David, come 'ere and sit down, you silly boy. You can show me the bedroom later.

DAVID. I say! (*He helps himself to another drink.*) Oh, sorry. (*He pours one for* MARIA *and hands it to her. She pats the couch invitingly.*) No, thanks, I've been sitting about all day.

MARIA. Oh, you English. Don't you ever let yourselves go?

DAVID. Well, I sing in the bath a bit.

MARIA (*reaching out and pulling him down beside her*). So. Is better, hmmm? (*She curls her fingers in his hair.*) What you say, eh?

DAVID (*feebly*). Help!

MARIA. Tell me about yourself.

DAVID (*giggling foolishly*). I say—ow! (*She has pulled a bit hard.*)

MARIA. When I first see you I am saying 'e is different, this one. Dark, 'andsome and strong. (DAVID *struggles to get away, but* MARIA *pulls him back again.*) Come, I read the future in your eyes. (*She takes his face between her hands.*) Look at me. (*Her voice has gone low and husky.*) Look into my eyes.

DAVID (*giggling again*). My nose gets in the way.

MARIA. I see all your 'idden thoughts. Ah. You are very passionate.

DAVID (*gazing vacantly at her*). Am I? (*His lips purse for a kiss and he leans perilously close.*)

MARIA. Now let me see your 'ands. (*She takes her hands away from his face suddenly and he all but falls into her lap. She seizes one of his hands and traces the lines with her long forefinger.*)

DAVID (*giggling*). You're tickling.

MARIA. Keep still. I see strange things. Oh, David, the 'eart line is very strong. You will love fiercely!

DAVID (*gazing enthralled into his other hand*). Good Lord! Will I really.

MARIA. And 'ere, what is this?

DAVID. A blister.

MARIA. No, no. It is a sign, but I cannot read it. (*She looks round the room.*) The light is too strong. I must 'ave soft lights.

DAVID (*eagerly*). Well, let's have the lamp on instead. (*He makes, a little unsteadily, for the door.*) You switch on and I'll put this one out. (*As* MARIA *reaches towards the table-lamp* DAVID *turns out the light, leaving the room in complete darkness.*)

MARIA (*in the darkness*). I cannot find the switch.

DAVID. Hang on a minute. I'll come and help.

MARIA. Is all right. I 'ave it.

(An ear-splitting roar begins; it is the vacuum-cleaner, which is still plugged into the lamp.)
(Screams.) David!

DAVID *(shouts)*. All right, all right, it's only the cleaner. I've got you.

(The lights come on again disclosing MARIA and DAVID clutching one another in mid-stage. In the open doorway, KATE with her hand on the light switch. She reacts violently to this tableau. DAVID, startled by the sudden illumination, attempts to look nonchalant while disengaging himself from MARIA, who shows no inclination to break up the party.

KATE, not deigning to shout over the noise of the cleaner, walks briskly across the room and switches off. As the cleaner gurgles into silence DAVID attempts a wan smile.)

Hello, Kate, old girl. Didn't expect to see you again so soon.

KATE. So I see. Oh, David, how could you?

DAVID. But, Katie darling—

KATE. Don't speak to me you—you satyr!

DAVID. But, I say, look here, you don't understand.

KATE. Oh, I hate you! *(She bursts into tears and throws herself on to the couch in misery.)*

(Enter MRS. SCOTT.)

MRS. SCOTT. Hello, David. Here we are again. You might have guessed it—a puncture. Oh, I didn't know you had company. How do you do? *(She shakes hands with MARIA.)* I'm Kate's mother. You've met David, I see.

MARIA. 'Ow do you do. I am Maria.

MRS. SCOTT. How nice. *(She moves to the couch.)* Kate dear, don't be unsociable.

KATE *(looking up with red eyes)*. Oh, Mother, how can you be so calm!

MRS. SCOTT. Well, dear, it's not the first puncture I've had and we were only doing forty—

KATE. But don't you understand? I found them here together with the lights out. They were making love!

DAVID *(shocked)*. I say, Kate!

KATE. It's no good, David. I never want to speak to you again.

MARIA. You are not understanding.

KATE. Don't you speak to me, you—you Jezebel!

MARIA. No, I am Maria.

MRS. SCOTT. Now, Kate, don't be unkind. I'm sure it's all very simple.

KATE *(jumping up)*. Oh, don't be so damned reasonable, Mother! They were making love in the middle of the room with the lights out and the vacuum-cleaner on.

MRS. SCOTT. How novel! Were you, David?

DAVID. Of course not.

MRS. SCOTT. There you are then, Kate. Now no more nonsense.

KATE. I tell you I saw them and (*Indicating* MARIA.)—well, look at her!

MRS. SCOTT. What a charming robe. Where did you get it, dear?

MARIA. Is all very simple. I will explain.

MRS. SCOTT. Good. And while we are listening I shall have a glass of that excellent brandy you have there, David. (*She settles herself comfortably in the easy-chair.*)

DAVID. Yes, of course. (*He busies himself with the bottle at the sideboard, giving himself a stiff one in the process.*)

MARIA. You see, I am Maria and David invite me because 'e is lonely.

KATE. Oh! (*She bursts into tears again and buries her head in her hands.*)

MARIA (*getting excited*). But you see 'is letters. 'E say you agree I come to keep 'im company while you are away.

KATE (*looking up*). What?

DAVID. Yes, old girl. I told you it was all right. (*He hands* MRS. SCOTT *a drink.*) You see, Mario turned out to be Maria, that's all. Small grammatical error. (*He returns to* C.)

KATE. You expect me to believe that?

MARIA. I am not understanding.

MRS. SCOTT. David thought you were a man, my dear.

MARIA (*menacingly to* DAVID). You think I am a man?

DAVID (*backing* R.). Yes, I mean, no. I did, but I don't.

MARIA (*temperamentally*). I am looking like a man?

DAVID. Good Lord no. Anything but!

KATE (*jumping up*). David!

DAVID. Oh, Lord! What I mean to say is—if I'd known what you were really like I wouldn't have dreamt of inviting you.

MARIA. Oh, David, after all you said!

KATE. There, Mother, you see?

MARIA (*to* KATE). But why are you so angry with your brother?

KATE. My what? (*Approaching* DAVID, *who stands near the table looking rather foolish.*) David, just what did you put in those letters?

DAVID. Well, you see, there's a page missing from my dictionary and I thought—

KATE. You wretch!

MARIA. You are not 'is sister?

KATE. No, I am not. I am 'is wife.

MARIA (*to* DAVID). You are a spouse?

KATE. Yes, only I spell it with an L.

MARIA (*advancing*). You are the bigamister.

DAVID. Now wait a minute!

KATE (*also advancing*). Bluebeard!

MARIA. Snake in the hay!

DAVID (*taking refuge behind the table*). No, no, let me explain.

MRS. SCOTT (*shouting above the din*). Children! (*Recovering her composure.*) Children! You seem to be unpopular, David.

DAVID. I couldn't be more miserable.

(*The telephone rings and* DAVID *stamps across and bellows into it.*) Hello!—Oh, I beg your pardon. (*Whispers.*) Hello. Yes, this is Wild Green 5892—You what?—my call to where?—Oh, Naples— Naples! Hey, wait a minute—there's a mistake!

MARIA (*snatching the phone from him*). Is for me. 'Allo, 'allo. *Pronto, pronto.—Carlo?—Ah mio caro—* (*She curls up on the couch and the rest is murmured unheard into the telephone. Her call continues throughout the ensuing scene.*)

DAVID (*to* MRS. SCOTT). How much is a call to Italy?

MRS. SCOTT. Oh about five pounds a minute, I should think.

DAVID. And the phone bill due next month!

(*There is a violent knocking on the door and two pictures fall.* DAVID *stamps across and opens the door to disclose the* CURATE.)

What the devil do you want? (*Noticing his collar.*) Oh! Holy Moses!

CURATE. Aha. Flattery, flattery. I'm only the curate. I called to see whether you would care to subscribe to our little fund. (*He holds up his collecting-tin.*) It's Good Fellowship Week, you know.

DAVID. Oh, go to hell! (*He stops short and sniffs.*) What's that smell of burning? (*He rushes to open the kitchen door and is met by a cloud of smoke.*) Oh, Lord, I forgot the kettle. (*He disappears inside.* KATE *picks up a soda siphon and directs it towards the kitchen. There is a yell and* DAVID *reappears holding a smoking kettle with a gaping hole in the bottom.*) Look what's happened to my bottom!

(KATE *squirts him liberally with the siphon and the* CURATE *beats a hasty retreat.*)

QUICK CURTAIN

ACT TWO

SCENE I

The same, late that night. When the curtain rises the stage is in darkness. A clock strikes two. The entrance door opens slowly and a figure is seen in silhouette against a light outside. It slips into the flat and closes the door. There is a bump and muffled cursing. After a moment or two there is a sneeze followed by rustling.

MARIA. 'Allo? 'Oo is it?

(The table-lamp is switched on, disclosing MARIA sitting up on the couch which has been converted into a bed. She clutches the clothes round her and is clearly uncomfortable. There is no sign of the intruder.)

Cellini?

(Silence. After listening a moment she takes the little package out of her handbag and hides it under her pillow. She shivers suddenly.)

Is very cold.

(She counts the blankets.)

One—two. Oh these cold-bedded English!

(She sits thoughtfully for a moment or two then slips out of bed and pulls on her négligée and slippers. She disappears into the kitchen with her handbag. This is the signal for the burglar to appear. He rises, complete with mask, cap and striped shirt from behind the couch and, having first ensured that MARIA is safely in the kitchen, goes to work on the sideboard. As soon as he speaks we recognize the TAXI-DRIVER from Act One.

He is somewhat distracted by the array of bottles on the sideboard and seizing the nearest takes a hearty swig.)

BURGLAR *(spluttering)*. Gawd strewth! 'E must be a chemist.

(He listens intently with the bottle still in his hand. There is a noise from the bathroom and he rushes to the bed, dropping the bottle on the floor nearby, and burrows under the clothes. The bathroom door opens and DAVID appears, pyjama-clad, sleepy and miserable. He has a short blanket draped round his shoulders. He blinks in the light and advances a little way into the room.)

DAVID *(in a loud whisper)*. I say, Maria, you awake?

(There is no response.)

I saw the light and thought perhaps you couldn't sleep either.

(A loud and unconvincing snore from the couch.)

Good Lord. Adenoids!

(He moves round the room stamping and flapping.)

It's beastly cold.

> (*He tries to warm his hands at the lamp and continues conversationally.*)

They only gave me one blanket. I ask you! One blanket in a bath. I don't know whether to put it under me or over me. Talk about frozen assets! And the tap drips on my feet.

> (*He sits on the edge of the couch.*)

I'll bet it's warm in there!

> (*There is a commotion under the clothes and the* BURGLAR's *voice is heard, disguised and squeaky.*)

BURGLAR. Go away!

> (DAVID *jumps up and regards the hump under the clothes in some surprise.*)

DAVID. What?

BURGLAR. Go away!

DAVID. Oh, all right. (*He starts back to the bathroom, stops, scratches his head and returns.*) I say?

BURGLAR. Yes?

DAVID. Are you all right? You sound sort of funny.

BURGLAR. I've gotta ze cold. Go away.

DAVID. All right. I say, I suppose you haven't got a spare blanket you don't want?

> (*A bare and very hairy arm emerges and plucks at the top blanket.*)

I say, you're a sport, Maria. (*He takes the blanket and wraps himself up like a Red Indian.*) Sure you don't mind?

BURGLAR. No. Go away.

DAVID. Good night then. Sleep tight. (*He steps back and nearly falls over the bottle, now empty. He picks it up and sniffs at it.*) Very tight by the looks of it. Who'd have thought it?

> (*He suddenly catches sight of the arm, which is still uncovered. He pulls out one of the hairs experimentally and it immediately disappears under the clothes.* DAVID *sniffs at the bottle again with renewed interest and shrugs.*)

I wonder if Auntie ever thought of selling it as hair restorer?

> (*Shaking his head sadly, he places the bottle on the coffee-table, which is drawn up beside the couch, and returns to the bathroom. The* BURGLAR's *head emerges from the clothes.* DAVID *turns, but he has ducked down again just in time.* DAVID *comes back and switches off the light.*)

Good night.

> (*The bathroom door opens and closes and* DAVID *has gone. The* BURGLAR *sits up and turns the light on again.*)

BURGLAR. Strewth! Nearly 'ad to defend me 'onour. Sorry to disappoint you, mate. (*He looks at the closed bathroom door.*) Funny place to sleep. I suppose 'e keeps a pet loofah in 'is bed. Now where's that 'andbag? (*He looks under the couch and then continues his search round the room on all fours. While he is poking about behind the couch a noise from the kitchen disturbs him. He looks up and listens.*) Proper Piccadilly Circus this is.

(*He bobs down out of sight as* MARIA *enters from the kitchen with a glass of milk in one hand and a car-rug in the other. She puts the milk down on the coffee-table, spreads the rug over the couch and climbs in. She snuggles down in her négligée, but sits up again with a curious expression on her face. She counts the blankets again.*)

MARIA. One—two? Is not possible!

(*She leans out and looks all round for the missing cover, notices the empty bottle, picks it up and sniffs it. The bathroom door opens again and* DAVID *appears still wrapped in his blanket.*)

DAVID (*seeing* MARIA *with the bottle*). Aha! Strong stuff, eh? Feeling better? Hair of the dog, eh?

MARIA. I am not understanding. What dog?

DAVID. Don't worry. I won't breathe a word. I must say you look pretty good considering.

MARIA. Considering what?

DAVID. Oh, you know. Bottoms up and all that. Old Auntie would be bucked.

MARIA. David, we've 'ad a difficult day. I am tired and cold and I am not wishing to talk nonsense.

DAVID. Thick head, eh?

(*While this has been going on the* BURGLAR *has been creeping on all fours towards the front door.*)

(*Spotting her glass of milk, but not seeing the* BURGLAR.) Hallo! What have we here?

(*The* BURGLAR, *still unnoticed, scuttles back behind the couch.*)
Where did you get that?

MARIA. I warmed it up in the kitchen. I was going to drink it (DAVID *sits down on the couch.*)—and go to sleep!

DAVID (*disappointed*). Oh! (*He jumps up again.*) I think I'll have the same. It doesn't seem to take long to boil. (*He goes to the kitchen—his head reappears.*) Thanks for the blanket. (*Goes out.*)

MARIA. The blanket?

(*She springs out of bed and approaches the kitchen.*)
(*Calling.*) You are a low-down blanket-thiever. I get my own back.

(*She rushes to the bathroom and disappears inside. The* BURGLAR *jumps up and locks her in.* MARIA *begins to beat on the door and shout.*)
(*Off.*) David, let me out! You are a beast. I 'ate you! David— David.

BURGLAR (*in a loud whisper*). 'Ere, put a damper on it, mate. You'll
'ave 'em all out of bed.

    (*The banging continues and he loses his temper and bangs back and
shouts.*)

Shurrup!

    (MARIA *stops banging and the* BURGLAR *makes his way on tip-toe
towards the front door. But this time he is headed off by a noise from the
bedroom and scuttles back to the couch and clambers in.*)

Cor! Another of 'em. I would 'ave to pick on a 'ouseful of insomni-
maniacs.

    (*He disappears under the covers as* KATE *enters. She is wearing a
dressing-gown. Cautiously she creeps to the bed, sits on the edge of the
couch and addresses the hump under the clothes.*)

KATE. Maria?

    (*No reply.*)

It's no good pretending to be asleep because I heard you creeping
about just now.

    (*No response.*)

All right then, if you must sulk. You can still listen to what I want to
say. I've been thinking over what happened and I've decided I may
have been a bit hasty last night. I—

    (MARIA *rattles the bathroom door and then resumes her banging.*)

Damn! David's awake. (*In a loud whisper.*) Do be quiet, David;
you'll wake everyone up.

    (*More knocking.*)

All right, all right. I'm coming.

    (*She goes to the bathroom door.*)

Hallo, it's locked.

    (*She smiles wickedly towards the couch and unlocks the door.*)

You're more suspicious of him than I am!

    (MARIA *bursts out with a blanket round her shoulders.*)

Maria! (*She is thunderstruck.*)

MARIA. 'Ow dare you lock me in!

KATE. How dare you go near my husband.

MARIA. I don' wanna go near 'im. 'E steala my blanket.

    (*She stares with* KATE *at the hump on the couch.*)

Oh!

KATE. And now he's after bigger game.

MARIA. I am not knowing.

KATE. Oh, you wouldn't notice if an elephant got in bed. Too naïve
for words.

MARIA. I am not the knave. It is 'im. 'E is a blanket-thiever.

(A fit of coughing from under the blankets interrupts this dialogue. As they watch a hairy arm emerges, seizes MARIA's *glass of milk and conveys it under the covers. A few moments later it reappears with an empty glass.)*

And now 'e drinka my milk.

KATE *(bursting into tears)*. Oh, David. After all you promised.

(She rushes off to the bedroom. MARIA *sits on the couch and addresses the occupant.)*

MARIA. David, you are a bad boy and upsetting Kate. I know it is only in joke—

*(*DAVID *enters from the kitchen with a glass of milk.)*

but is very late and I am tired. Please go back to your bath.

DAVID *(from behind her)*. Right-ho! Just going.

MARIA *(turns and nearly screams)*. David! I am bewitching!

DAVID. Hear! Hear!

MARIA *(pointing to the hump on the couch)*. Then who—who?

DAVID. You sound like an owl. *(Seeing the couch and its burden.)* I say, what have you got there? What's Kate doing in your bed?

MARIA *(whispers)*. Is not Kate. *(She takes refuge behind him.)*

DAVID. Then who the devil is it?

MARIA. I thought it was you.

DAVID. No, I don't think so—unfortunately.

MARIA. David, I'm frightened.

DAVID. There, there. *(He puts down his glass of milk and puts an arm manfully round her shoulders.)* I'll soon settle this. *(He addresses the couch.)* Hey there! You in bed. *(He prods the lump.)* I say, you can't sleep there, you know. *(Getting no response, he gingerly pulls the coverlet back, exposing the* BURGLAR's *masked face. Hurriedly he covers it up again.)* Good Lord, a highwayman! *(He picks up his glass of milk and makes for the front door.)*

MARIA *(chasing after him)*. David, don't leave me!

DAVID. That's all right. Just keep an eye on him. I'll get the police.

(At this word the BURGLAR *sits up and points a gun at them.)*

MARIA *(screaming)*. He's got a gun!

DAVID. Good Lord. He's gone to bed with his hat on!

BURGLAR *(gruffly)*. Stick 'em up.

DAVID. I can't stick 'em up. I shall spill my milk.

BURGLAR. Stick one of 'em up then.

*(*DAVID *does so and the* BURGLAR *clambers off the couch.)*

MARIA. I know 'im. 'E drive me 'ere in a taxi.

DAVID. A tall, dark, handsome cabbie, eh?

BURGLAR. You be careful. I ain't in no mood for jokes.

DAVID *(one hand still in the air)*. Please, teacher?

BURGLAR. No, you can't!

DAVID. But this milk is burning my hand. Here, you hold it.
>   (*He hands the glass to* MARIA.)

MARIA. Ow! Is hot. 'Ere.
>   (*She hands it to the* BURGLAR, *who juggles with it and his gun.*
> DAVID *takes his gun to help him out.*)

DAVID. Half a minute.
>   (*He takes a handkerchief from his pocket and wraps it round his
> hand, takes back the milk and gives the* BURGLAR *back his gun.*)

BURGLAR. Orl right. Stick it up again.
>   (DAVID *does.*)

>   (*During the next speech the* BURGLAR *turns his back on them and
> walks across stage spinning the gun on his finger cowboy-fashion. They
> creep towards him, but he turns suddenly and they back away again.*)

I ain't never come across a 'ouse like this in me life. Tramp, tramp,
tramp all night. It ain't decent. I 'aven't spent so much time 'opping
in and out of bed since me 'oneymoon.

DAVID. I say, are you married?

MARIA. 'E 'as four children.

DAVID. Yes, I dare say. But—

BURGLAR. Why do you think I started this lark? Me ol' woman snores.

MARIA. But what are you going to do?

BURGLAR. Me? I'm going to scarper before the rest of the 'ouse comes
in for a spot of twisting. (*To* DAVID.) You and yer bit of fluff get in
there. (*He motions towards the bathroom.*)

DAVID. But it's cold in there.

BURGLAR. Then drink yer 'ot milk and 'ave a cuddle. Come on, look
sharp. I haven't got all night, you know.

>   (*Reluctantly they move towards the bathroom.*)

DAVID. Perhaps you wouldn't mind explaining the situation to my
wife. She might think—

BURGLAR. 'Op it!

>   (*He shepherds them into the bathroom and locks the door. He wipes
> his brow wearily.*)

'Ow do they expect a man to do an 'onest day's work keeping 'im up
all hours? I shall get bags under me mask. Now just in case anyone
gets worried. (*He arranges pillows under the clothes so that there appears
to be somebody in the couch. As he does so he finds the package.*) There
we are. Tucked up all warm and cosy. Night, night. 'Allo, 'allo,
what's all this? (*He holds the package up to the light, then shakes it near
his ear.*) Consolation prize. (*He stuffs it into his pocket, pats the lumps
in the bed and makes for the door, which starts to open as he approaches.
He dives back behind the couch.*)
Oh, gawd!

(Enter CELLINI. *He is middle-aged and, as we shall see later, is going bald. At present he wears hat, coat and white scarf, and carries a stick which could well turn out to be a sword stick. His English is good with an occasional lapse, his manners continental. This is, however, a façade. He creeps furtively forward and addresses the lump in the bed.)*

CELLINI *(whispers).* Maria. Maria. *(Louder.)* Maria! Is Cellini. *Maledetto!* Wake up, wake up. *(He shakes the pillow gently by the shoulder. It doesn't respond and he, too, spots the empty bottle and sniffs it.)* Little fool.

(He wanders round the room and when his back is turned the BURGLAR *bobs up, disappearing again as* CELLINI *turns. This happens two or three times until* CELLINI *returns to the couch and tries again.)*

Maria! Hey, Maria! I 'ave come for the diamonds.

(The BURGLAR *bobs up and down again highly excited.* CELLINI *pokes the pillow with his stick and gets no response.)*

Santa Maria! She musta be deada drunk.

(There is a loud bump on the bathroom door.)

Dio! Someone is coming. Maria, quick—the necklace. *Madre mia!* I cannot wait. I come back tomorrow.

(He beats a hasty retreat. No sooner has he gone than the BURGLAR *bobs up all agog, takes out the package and shakes it.)*

BURGLAR. Sparklers! Cor! Manna from 'eaven. *(He pats the lump in the bed again.)* Moochos grazios, Senorita.

(He makes his escape and closes the front door behind him just as KATE *and* MRS. SCOTT *enter from the bedroom.* MRS. SCOTT *is also in her dressing-gown.)*

MRS. SCOTT. But, Catherine, I really cannot see why you have to drag me out of bed in the middle of the night—

KATE. Because this time I want you to see for yourself. Look! *(She points at the couch.)*

MRS. SCOTT. Most interesting. Now can I go back to bed?

(She returns to the bedroom door. KATE *throws back the clothes and reveals the pillows.)*

KATE. Come on out, David. Oh! They must have gone off together.

MRS. SCOTT. Oh, really, Kate.

(There are thuds and scufflings from the bathroom.)

KATE. There, you see. What did I tell you? *(She unlocks the bathroom door.)* Come on out.

(Out come DAVID *and* MARIA, *looking just a shade sheepish.)*

Now do you believe me?

MRS. SCOTT *(coming forward).* Well, I must say you do choose odd times and places for a conversation, David.

DAVID. Has he gone?

MRS. SCOTT. Who, dear?

DAVID. The burglar.

MARIA. The taxi-driver. 'E was very fierce.

DAVID. Yes, 'e was.

MARIA. And David was very brave.

DAVID. Oh, I say, do you think so?

MARIA. 'E locked us in the bathroom with 'is gun.

MRS. SCOTT. How exciting.

KATE (*moving* D.L.). I'm not falling for that one. I've forgiven you once, David, but this is too much. (*Virtuously.*) A girl can bear just so much.

DAVID. That's what I thought until I went to that little night club off Piccadilly!

KATE. We're not interested in your lurid sex-life. You can keep that for your other women. (*With a glance at* MARIA.) They don't seem to have any taste.

DAVID. But, Katie—

KATE (*shouting*). Oh, I could scratch her eyes out!

MRS. SCOTT. Control, Catherine, control!

DAVID. Yes, dear, remember Maria is our guest.

KATE. You shut up.

DAVID. Katie!

KATE. Well, how can I be calm with her standing there like a trollop?

MARIA. What is a trollop?

DAVID. Oh—it's a sort of fish. Take no notice.

MARIA (*angrily*). She is calling me a fish? (*To* KATE, *shouting.*) And you are the stuck-up prig!

KATE. Pig?

MRS. SCOTT. No dear, prig.

KATE. Witch!

MARIA. *Basta!* Is enough. You are jealous because 'e like me. With a wife like you is no wonder 'e want a little comforting. (*She strokes* DAVID's *head.*) Poor David.

KATE. I'll give him poor David.
>(*There is a knock on the front door and the picture falls.*)
That damned picture! (*She runs to it and picks it up.*)

DAVID. Now don't be unkind to Psyche.

KATE. Oh! You and your women!
>(*She lifts it high and smashes it over his head. He collapses on the couch in a dazed condition.*)

MARIA. David! (*She runs to nurse him.*)

MRS. SCOTT. Children, children!

KATE (*dusting her hands*). Perhaps that'll cool your ardour.
>(*There is renewed knocking on the door and* MRS. MACWHIMBLE'S *voice is heard outside.*)

MRS. MAC (*off*). Mr. Abbott. Mr. Abbott! I will not 'ave this rumpus.

KATE. Oh dear. It's the dragon.

MRS. SCOTT. Leave this to me. Quick, clear away the evidence.

> (KATE *and* MARIA *take* DAVID *by the arms and steer him complete with his picture necklace into the bathroom.*)

MRS. MAC (*off*). Do you 'ear me? Open the door.

MRS. SCOTT. Now into the bathroom with you—and don't fight.

> (KATE *and* MARIA *glare at one another and fly into the bathroom as* MRS. SCOTT *climbs into the bed and picks up a book.*)

MRS. MAC (*off, hammering on the door*). Open up, I say.

MRS. SCOTT. Come in. It's not locked. Unfortunately.

> (*Enter* MRS. MACWHIMBLE *in voluminous night attire, her hair in a long pigtail. She carries a large poker.*)

Oh, good evening.

MRS. MAC. Evening! It's nigh on three o'clock in the morning.

MRS. SCOTT. Really? This is such a fascinating book I lose all sense of time. It's called—er—(*She consults the title and turns it up the right way.*) Accidence and Syntax in the Fifth Form. (*Hurriedly.*) It's all about teenage love.

MRS. MAC (*peering round*). Where are they 'iding?

MRS. SCOTT. Who?

MRS. MAC. Why, all the others, of course. You weren't making all that row by yerself, I'm sure.

MRS. SCOTT. Row? You must have been dreaming.

MRS. MAC. I was not!

MRS. SCOTT. Won't you sit down?

MRS. MAC. No, I won't! Not at this unchristian hour. And what are you still 'ere for anyway?

MRS. SCOTT. I had a puncture.

MRS. MAC. I dare say you did. But that don't prevent you from sitting in a train, does it?

MRS. SCOTT. It depends where you get the puncture.

MRS. MAC. Hmph! Well, you've nearly punctured my ceiling with your goings on.

MRS. SCOTT. I suppose you don't suffer from noises in the head?

MRS. MAC. Not so as I've noticed.

MRS. SCOTT. Noises like voices shouting and pictures breaking?

MRS. MAC. Why, now you come to mention it, that's just what it did sound like.

MRS. SCOTT (*very solemnly*). Then you really ought to go and lie down, my dear. I've heard of people in your condition who just dropped down like that. One minute lively as a cricket, the next (*She snaps her fingers.*)—out!

MRS. MAC. You don't say. (*She sits down by the table.*) Come to think of it, that's just what 'appened to my old man.
MRS. SCOTT. You see? You can't be too careful at your age, my dear, with noises in the head.
MRS. MAC. Yers. 'E was took just like that. Didn't even 'ave time to finish the bottle afore 'e went.
MRS. SCOTT. How tragic.
MRS. MAC. I'm glad you told me. I might 'ave been took bad all unbeknownst.
MRS. SCOTT. If I were you I should go straight back to bed.
MRS. MAC. (*shaking her head sadly*). Yes, I will. 'Oo'd 'ave thought it? (*She totters carefully towards the door, turns and is about to speak.*)
MRS. SCOTT. Remember! (*She snaps her fingers.*)
MRS. MAC. Yes, yes, like that.

> (*She opens the door and is about to leave when the bathroom door opens and DAVID staggers out still wearing his picture and carrying his glass of milk. He is hotly pursued by the two girls.*)

DAVID. I say, you know, this milk has gone cold.

QUICK CURTAIN

SCENE 2

The same. Breakfast-time next morning. The table has been drawn out from the wall and is laid for four. The couch has returned to normal, but is piled high with bedclothes. Otherwise the room is very much as it was for Act One, except, of course, for a space where Psyche once hung.

> MRS. SCOTT *is knitting quietly on the couch. Enter* KATE *from the kitchen, very tight-lipped, with a jug of milk which she bangs down on the table. She and* MRS. SCOTT *are fully dressed.*

MRS. SCOTT. Anything I can do, dear?
KATE. No, thank you. (*She stands back and surveys the table.*) I think that's about the lot. Powdered glass in the sugar basin and arsenic in the coffee. You haven't got a stiff dose of cyanide in your handbag, I suppose?
MRS. SCOTT. Don't be silly, dear. Just pour me out a nice cup of tea and calm down. It's really not David's fault, you know.
KATE. Hmph! (*She pours out a cup of tea.*)
MRS. SCOTT. Two lumps, please (KATE *drops in two lumps from a great height.*) Thank you. I think Maria is rather a sweet girl.
KATE (*holding out a plate of eggs*). Hard-boiled!

MRS. SCOTT. What, dear? Oh, no, thank you. Just a slice of toast for me. You carry on.

KATE. I'm not hungry.

MRS. SCOTT. Really, Kate, you must have something.

KATE. I couldn't, Mother. I've got a headache. Anyway, the toast is burnt.

MRS. SCOTT. Now, Catherine, I hope you're not going to be difficult.

KATE. Of course not. It's all very straightforward.

MRS. SCOTT. Good.

KATE. Either she goes today or I do. David must choose between us.

MRS. SCOTT. Oh dear. You know he has such odd tastes.

KATE (*toying with a spoon*). Mother! I can't go on like this.

MRS. SCOTT. Good. And if you must be so tragic about it stop waving the egg-spoon.

KATE. Oh, Mother, I'm so wretched.

MRS. SCOTT. Yes, dear. Could I have my tea, do you think? Where is David, by the way? (KATE *comes across with the tea and toast and indicates the bedroom.*)

KATE. He's lying on the bed with the curtains drawn, pretending to feel ill. Serve him right.

MRS. SCOTT. Kate, you're getting positively spiteful.

KATE (*back to the table and sits facing the audience*). And she is having a bath, if you please!

MRS. SCOTT. And a very good principle, too. When in hot water take a bath. (*She puts down her tea and goes to the bedroom door, carrying her toast.*) David! David dear, breakfast! (*She returns to the couch, nibbling at her toast.*) The trouble is, Kate, you take things far too seriously.

KATE. Well, isn't it serious? David's practically living in sin under my very nose—

MRS. SCOTT. How unhygienic!

KATE. Mrs. MacWhimble's given us a week's notice and—and I've burnt the toast. I just don't understand how it all happened.

MRS. SCOTT. You probably had the gas too high.

KATE. Oh, Mother, do be serious.

MRS. SCOTT. Nonsense! It's such a lovely day—much too nice to be serious. Let's do something gay. What about a picnic?

KATE. Oh, no!

        (*Her voice falters as she sees* DAVID, *who has entered from the bedroom. He is unshaven, unwashed and looks thoroughly disreputable. He is wearing a dressing-gown.*)

MRS. SCOTT. Good morning, David dear. Sleep well?

DAVID. 'Morning. (*He yawns prodigiously and stretches.*) Didn't sleep a wink.

(*Tentatively he approaches* KATE *from behind. She sits glaring savagely at the teapot.*)
Good morning, darling.
(*Getting no reply, he tries again by kissing the back of her neck. She shrugs him off angrily.*)
I seem to be very popular this morning. Did I forget to wipe the blood off my hands?

MRS. SCOTT. Never mind, dear. Kate doesn't feel quite herself this morning.

DAVID (*sitting* D.S.R. *and attacking a boiled egg*). I feel pretty awful, too!

KATE. Ha!

DAVID. I'm glad somebody cares. Since you ask, it's like a piece of sandpaper under each eyelid. Lack of sleep.

KATE. No need to boast about it.

DAVID (*sniffing suspiciously*). I say, this egg's bad.

MRS. SCOTT. It should be all right, it's got a little lion on it.

DAVID. That's not a lion, it's a sphinx—and it stinx!

KATE. That's right, criticize! I suppose I don't know how to boil an egg now? (*She begins to pile the breakfast things on to a tray on the table.*)

DAVID. It didn't need boiling. It needed fumigating. Here, I say!
(*He rescues his plate from* KATE.)

MRS. SCOTT (*rising*). Well, if you two are on speaking terms again, I'll go and prepare a hamper.

DAVID. What's that about a hamper?

MRS. SCOTT. We're going on a picnic. A day in the open air.

DAVID. Oh Lord, what a ghastly idea!

KATE. It will do you the world of good. You're getting pimply.

DAVID. I am *not* pimply. (*He inspects himself in a spoon.*) Those are moles. Anyway, I'd sooner have pimples than be bitten to death by warble flies. (*Inevitably he pulls a face at himself in the spoon.*) I say, do look at this face.

KATE. I can see it.

MRS. SCOTT (*moving to the table and picking up some of the breakfast things*). That's settled then. I'll go and make some sandwiches. What shall we have in them?

DAVID. What about Maria?

KATE. Good idea—minced!

DAVID. No, I mean on the picnic. I think she's allergic to horse-flies.

MRS. SCOTT. Oh, nonsense. She would love a day in the country.

KATE. Personally I'm sorry for the horse-flies.

DAVID. Where is she, by the way?

KATE. In the bathroom. It has happy memories for her.

MRS. SCOTT. Now then, Catherine. Let bygones be bygones.

DAVID. Hear! Hear!

KATE. Pipe down, has-been.

MRS. SCOTT. And when you've finished breakfast you can help me
with the sandwiches.

(*She goes into the kitchen with dirty crocks.* DAVID *butters some
toast which he has grabbed back from the tray. It shatters at the first bite.*)

DAVID. The toast is burnt.

KATE. Well?

DAVID. I like burnt toast.

(*There is a momentary silence.*)

KATE. David?

DAVID. Hmmm?

KATE. You will send her away, won't you?

DAVID (*surprised*). Who? Mother? That's a bit hard-hearted, isn't it?

KATE. No, not Mother, you wretched man—Maria.

DAVID. But I say, she'll be frightfully disappointed. I mean, we did
invite her, after all.

KATE. You invited her—not me. And now you're telling her to go
home again. I'm serious, David. If you don't get rid of that sex-cat
today, I'm going off with Mother and I'm not coming back.

DAVID. But what about the picnic?

KATE. I mean it!

DAVID. Oh!

KATE (*who is in a way enjoying the situation*). Well?

DAVID (*brightly*). Oh well, it can't be helped. I'll just have to (*Suddenly
gloomy.*)—explain to Maria that—that— (*A pause.*) I suppose you
wouldn't like to tell her?

KATE. That's right, I wouldn't.

DAVID (*squaring his shoulders*). All right then. I'll do it!

KATE. Darling, I love you.

(*She throws her arms round his neck and kisses him.*)

DAVID. I say, mind the marmalade!

KATE. She'll be out in a minute. I'll go and help Mother in the kitchen.
(*She gathers up the tray of dirty breakfast things.*) Be firm, darling.

(*She kisses him on the forehead and goes into the kitchen.* DAVID
*rises and paces up and down for a few moments with his chin stuck out and
resolution in every worried wrinkle.*)

DAVID. Firm! (*He addresses the table-lamp in a fatherly tone.*) Now,
my dear, you must be brave.

(*The bathroom door opens at this stage and discloses* MARIA *in
another daring and disarming négligée.*)

(*Backing away,* D.L.) Oh Lord—so must I!

MARIA. 'Allo, David. Is a beautiful morning.

DAVID (*still backing*). Yes, isn't it? Just the day for a picnic.

MARIA. Ah—is a lovely idea.

DAVID (*alarmed*). No, I meant to say a journey—a nice long journey.

MARIA (*moving to the table*). 'Ow funny you are, David. Nobody is going anywhere today. What is for breakfast?

DAVID (*absently*). Burnt egg and boiled toast.

MARIA (*sitting L. of the table with a shudder*). 'Orrible! Is an old English custom?

DAVID. Came over with the Conqueror. So did the eggs. (*He moves to* c.) Er—Maria—

MARIA. Did you know you 'ave smoke coming out from under your bath?

DAVID. Yes, isn't it novel? Maria—

MARIA. Is like a cannibal's pot.

DAVID. Yes, I know, but you must—

MARIA (*waving her marmalade knife dramatically*). Oh, David, I do like it 'ere.

DAVID. Oh Lord!

MARIA. Is a pity you are married, but never mind.

DAVID (*desperately*). Look, Maria, there's something I must say.

MARIA. Yes, David?

DAVID. I—well—how can I put it? You see how things are between Kate and me.

MARIA. But yes, my poor David, she is verree angree.

DAVID (*with apparent irrelevance*). And, dash it, I can't go on sleeping in the bath for ever.

MARIA. But no!

DAVID. It's so frustrating!

MARIA. Poor David!

DAVID. So I thought perhaps you—er—I, well—um—perhaps we could come to some other arrangement.

MARIA. Ah, David, now I know what you are thinking.

DAVID (*relieved*). You do? Thank heavens.

MARIA (*wagging her finger at him*). You are the dark 'orse. You play 'ard to get and then when a girl is unsuspicious you make the proposition.

DAVID. Well, I thought—you know—as you were so cold last night, perhaps you wouldn't mind a change. It can't have been much fun for you on that old couch. Anything's better than that—what?

MARIA. Anything? You English! You make the romance over a boiled egg.

DAVID (*baffled*). What?

MARIA. Is another old English custom?

DAVID. Yes, I expect so. I know it's asking a lot, but would you, just to oblige me?

MARIA (*huskily*). What would Katie say?

DAVID. Why she'd be delighted! I—

MARIA. What!

DAVID. I mean I'm sure she would understand. Of course, if it's a question of money—

MARIA. You makea the insult!

DAVID. Oh Lord, I've said the wrong thing.

MARIA. What kind of girl do you think I am, eh?

DAVID. A jolly nice one.

MARIA. But you makea me the insult!

DAVID. I'm sorry, honest I am.

MARIA. All right, then—but no more about the money.

  (*He looks thoroughly crestfallen and sits in the easy-chair to mop his brow. She comes over and sits on the arm of the chair, ruffling his hair.*)

David, you silly boy. You are worrying in case I am angree with you. There is no need. I am quite understanding.

DAVID (*relieved*). You are?

MARIA. Of course. You don't need to apologize.

DAVID. Oh good!

MARIA. I suppose I am—'ow you say—flattened.

DAVID. Oh, I wouldn't say that!

MARIA. No, no—flattered.

DAVID (*doubtfully*). You are?

MARIA. Yes, is nice for a girl to be desired.

DAVID. I say!

MARIA. But we must behave, for Katie's sake.

DAVID (*jumping up thoroughly alarmed*). Yes, but look here—

MARIA. No, David, is no good. Katie is your wife. I am understanding, but you must be a good boy.

DAVID. But—oh Lord!

MARIA. Now we will not talk about it any more. Where are we going for the picnic?

DAVID. Near the river, I hope. Then I can jump in!

MARIA (*rising*). We are swimming, too? You will like my costume—is very exciting. A one and a 'alf piece. (*She demonstrates the dimensions.*)

DAVID (*desperately*). Maria, listen to me. Wouldn't it be better to go away? It would make things so much easier for both of us.

MARIA. You are offering me the elopement? Is sweet of you, but very naughty. No, no, no, you wicked boy! (*She taps him playfully on the hand.*)

DAVID. Oh, what's the use? (*Calling.*) Katie!

KATE (*off*). Coming.

MARIA. Poor David.

(*Enter* KATE, *looking inquiringly from* DAVID *to* MARIA.)

KATE. Well?

DAVID (*shaking his head*). Unwell!

KATE. Oh, here, let me do it. (*She takes* MARIA *by the arm and leads her* D.R.) About this plan of David's—

MARIA (*rather taken aback*). I don't think I should—

KATE. Oh, that's all right. I know all about it. As a matter of fact, it was my idea.

DAVID (*wandering* D.L. *singing to himself*). You don't know what you're saying!

MARIA. Your idea!

KATE (*to* DAVID). Will you be quiet? (*To* MARIA.) But I thought it would sound better coming from David.

MARIA. Oh, yes, much better.

KATE. I suppose he told you our suggestion.

MARIA. Yes, indeed. He was being very suggestive.

KATE. But perhaps he didn't express himself very well.

MARIA. Oh, I know what his idea was!

KATE. Well then, you agree?

MARIA (*puzzled*). To David's suggestion?

KATE. Of course. Yes.

MARIA (*angrily*). You think I am the kind of girl 'oo—

DAVID. Kate, do let me explain.

KATE. Oh, go and make a pot of tea.

DAVID. There's still some left.

KATE. David, wasn't that Mother calling?

DAVID. I didn't hear her.

KATE (*loudly*). Will you go away!

DAVID. All right, all right. I can take a hint. Only I do wish you would let me explain.

(KATE *takes a step towards him.*)

I'm going, I'm going! (*He goes into the kitchen, shaking his head sadly.*)

KATE. Now, Maria—

MARIA. Mrs. Abbott—Kate—. Now we are alone I must tell you. I could not say anything to David, because I am 'urting 'is feelings.

KATE. That's nothing to what I should like to do to him.

MARIA. After all that 'as 'appened I cannot stay 'ere.

KATE (*astonished*). What?

MARIA. Is so. Yesterday I speak to my friend in Italy.

KATE. Yes?

MARIA. Is Carlo.

KATE (*politely*). Oh, yes?

MARIA. 'E is my fancy.

KATE. Fancy. Oh, fiancé! But I thought—

MARIA. Yes, 'e is worried I am being, 'ow you say, mizzled.

KATE. Mizzled? Oh, misled— Well what does he propose to do about it?

MARIA. 'E say—er—come 'ome at once.

KATE. What a wonderful idea—I mean, oh dear! But I can't think why he ever let you come alone in the first place.

MARIA. Oh, we are 'aving a lover's tuff. Is silly.

KATE. Not at all, perfectly natural.

MARIA. And now I am worrying that David will be upset if I go back.

KATE. Just you leave David to me.

MARIA. Is all right then?

KATE (*putting her arms round* MARIA'*s shoulders*). Is perfect.

MARIA. Good. Then I am 'appy again. I will go and pack.
      (*She goes into bedroom.* KATE *grins in delight and calls.*)

KATE. Oh, David!
          (DAVID'*s head appears cautiously from the kitchen.* KATE *beckons him into the room.*)

DAVID. Hallo, old girl. (*He looks round suspiciously.*) Er—everything all right?

KATE (*busily tidying the breakfast-table*). Of course. We have talked things over woman to woman (DAVID *winces.*)—and she agrees to do as you suggest.

DAVID (*aghast*). Yes, but, I say, look here. She misunderstood what I had in mind.

KATE. I doubt it! Anyway, she agrees to go away—

DAVID. Yes, but—

KATE (*walking into kitchen with crocks*).—back to her fancy.

DAVID. Yes, I know but— (*A shocked pause.*) What did you say?

KATE (*re-entering*). Her fiancé. He lives in Italy, you know.

DAVID. He does?

                    (KATE *nods.*)

    Good Lord!

KATE. Disappointed?

DAVID. Yes! I mean no—I mean—Good Lord!

KATE (*moving across with the remains of the crocks*). And you, my lad, are going to get freshened up before she leaves.

DAVID. Is she going as soon as that?

KATE. She certainly is. Hot-foot to save her virtue. Your reputation gets around, my chick-a-biddy. (*She chucks him under the chin and passes to the kitchen door.*) She thinks you're planning to mizzle her.

DAVID. Eh?

KATE. Come on—bathroom. I expect there's still some hot water left. (*She goes into kitchen.*)

DAVID (*puzzled*). I've never mizzled anyone in my life. (*Moving towards the bathroom.*) I just can't believe it. A girl like that—engaged!

KATE (*re-entering*). Tragic, isn't it. Now I promised to go round to the
garage and collect Mother's car. Oh, by the way, I've decided not to
visit Granny after all. It's not safe. (*She starts towards the door, but
stops short.*) Oh, my goodness, the picnic!

DAVID. What about it?

KATE. Well, we can't have one if Maria's going.

DAVID. That's a blessing, anyway. (*He mopes off into the bathroom and
closes the door.*)

KATE (*calling towards the kitchen*). Mummy dear, there's no need to make
any sandwiches, after all.

> (*She goes to the mirror and titivates her hair. MRS. SCOTT enters
> from the kitchen with an enormous heap of sandwiches on a plate.*)

MRS. SCOTT. There, that's done. What did you say, dear?

KATE (*in the doorway*). I said we shan't need any sandw—(*Turning and
catching sight of the heap.*) Oh dear!

MRS. SCOTT. Well, really, dear, I do think you might have told me.
My spreading finger's quite worn out.

KATE. Sorry, darling, but something just cropped up.

MRS. SCOTT. What about all these?

KATE. Oh, I expect they'll come in useful. I'm just going round to
collect the car. 'Bye now.

> (*She kisses her mother on the forehead and goes out, leaving MRS.
> SCOTT shaking her head sadly.*)

MRS. SCOTT. This reminds me of the first time I cooked a Sunday
dinner. We had brussel-sprout sandwiches for weeks. (*She samples
one and talks with her mouth full.*) David, David! Wherever are you,
dear?

> (*DAVID's head appears round the bathroom door.*)

Oh, there you are. Would you like a sandwich?

DAVID. But I'm just getting into the bath.

MRS. SCOTT. That's all right. They're water-cress.

> (*DAVID reaches out a bare arm and takes one.*)

DAVID. Thank you.

MRS. SCOTT (*looking beyond him into the bathroom*). It's very steamy in
there, dear. Your clothes will get damp. Let me have them and I'll
put them on a chair.

> (*DAVID disappears and his pyjamas and dressing-gown come flying
> out. The door closes. MRS. SCOTT folds them and puts them on the
> chair immediately outside the bathroom.*)

Now let me see what can I do with the rest? There now. (*She pats the
heap of clothes and picks up the plate of sandwiches.*) I wonder whether
Mrs. MacWhimble has any use for them.

(*She goes to the front door. MARIA appears from the bedroom, carrying a heap of her underclothes.*)

Oh, there you are. I'm just going to find out if dragons are vegetarians.

(*She goes out, sampling another sandwich. MARIA looks round for a suitable place to leave her clothes, spots the chair by the bathroom and moves DAVID's clothes to make room for her own. She throws DAVID's garments unceremoniously over the back of the couch. The telephone rings and she goes to answer it.*)

MARIA (*into phone*). 'Allo?—Cellini! You should not 'ave called me 'ere. Is too dangerous.—*Che?*—Of course I still 'ave it—But you never came.—No, I was not drunk—Yes, yes, is quite safe—*Che?*—Oh all right, *momento!*

(*She puts down the phone and looks under the pillow which is undermost on the couch. Finding nothing, she searches more desperately, then rushes back to the phone.*)

'Allo, 'allo—Cellini—is not there—No!—you must 'ave taken it—·I tell you no! Well, then someone 'as stolen it. —What?—No, I am not doing ze double-cross!—But listen—'Ere? You must not come 'ere. 'Allo, 'allo. (*She clicks the receiver violently then slams it down.*) *Madre mia!* 'E is mad. But it must be 'ere.

(*She scrabbles desperately on all sides of the couch, but in vain. The door-bell rings and she almost screams.*)

Impossible!

(*She goes to the door and throws it open. Enter MRS. BOTTLE. She is large, shapeless and common. About 50, but looking older, she wears blue overalls and a cloth cap and carries a bag of tools. She comes to C. a trifle aggressively.*)

MRS. BOTTLE. 'Mornin'.

MARIA. Good morning. I am thinking you are someone else.

MRS. BOTTLE. Oh? Well, I ain't. Me name's Bottle and I been a Bottle for thirty years.

MARIA. Oh!

MRS. BOTTLE. Yurs. I gave up a lot when I married Mr. Bottle.

MARIA. You did?

MRS. BOTTLE. Yurs. I used to be a Jugg. One of thirteen kids I was. Me Dad was an electrician and very well connected. (*She cackles with laughter.*) Now then. (*She takes out a large suction stick and sidles up to* MARIA.) Let's 'ave a look at your pipes.

MARIA (*alarmed*). What?

MRS. BOTTLE. Got trouble with 'em, 'aven't you?

(MARIA *looks bewildered.*)

You dunno what I'm talking about, do you?

MARIA. I am sorry.

MRS. BOTTLE. That's all right. I surprise a lot of people. You've 'eard of Alf Bottle, of course?

(MARIA *shakes her head.*)

No? Well, 'e's a plumber, see, and I'm Mrs. Bottle 'is old china. 'Is mate see? Plumber's mate.

(*She cackles with laughter, but* MARIA *remains nonplussed.*)

MARIA. A china plumber? You mend the plates?

MRS. BOTTLE. 'Ere, 'oo you kidding? Oh, never mind. Well, Mr. Bottle ain't well, see. Proper green bottle, 'e is. And 'e arsked if I'd come round and fix yer pipes like Mr. Abbott said.

MARIA. Oh, I see, I am sorry but (*Looking round.*)—they all seem to 'ave disappeared.

MRS. BOTTLE. Disappeared! Wot all of 'em?

MARIA. Yes.

MRS. BOTTLE. Wot about yer cistern?

MARIA (*puzzled*). She is in Italy.

MRS. BOTTLE. Italy! You know something? You got trouble 'ere. I'd best be getting to work straightaway. Where's the bathroom? I suppose you 'aven't sent yer bath to Spain for a 'oliday?

MARIA. No. Is in there—smoking. (*She indicates the bathroom.*)

MRS. BOTTLE. I 'ope it's old enough.

(*She cackles with laughter, picks up her bag of tools and then, confronted by the "Engaged" sign, looks inquiringly at* MARIA.)

MARIA. Is all right. It always says that.

(MRS. BOTTLE *almost opens the door, then turns back to* MARIA.)

MRS. BOTTLE. You did say yer bath was smoking?

MARIA. Yes.

MRS. BOTTLE. I suppose it ain't likely to burst into flames?

MARIA. No, I don't think so.

(MRS. BOTTLE *shrugs and marches resolutely into the bathroom, closing the door behind her.* MARIA *is just returning to the bedroom when a hoarse scream is heard.*)

MRS. BOTTLE (*off*). Ow my gawd!

DAVID (*off*). Help! Go away!

(*The bathroom door rattles wildly without obvious results.*)

MRS. BOTTLE (*off*). 'Elp. The door's jammed. 'Elp!

DAVID (*off*). Let me try.

MRS. BOTTLE (*off*). You stay where you are. 'Elp, 'elp, 'elp!

(*She hammers on the door.*)

MARIA (*trying the handle unsuccessfully*). Is stuck.

MRS. BOTTLE (*off*). Well, unstick it then!

(*More hammering on the door, followed by a knocking on the front door and ringing of the bell.* MARIA *stands* C. *irresolute for a moment and then runs quickly to the front door. She throws it open and practically embraces the new arrival, who, after a moment of struggle, succeeds in disengaging himself and is revealed as the* CURATE, *complete with large clerical hat and pince-nez.*)

MARIA. 'Elp, quickly.

CURATE. God bless my soul! My dear young lady. Good gracious. Er—get thee behind me—er—madam.

MARIA. 'Oo are you?

CURATE. My name is Fortescue, Cuthbert Fortescue. I came to see Mr. Abbott. Is he engaged?

   (*There is a renewed banging from the bathroom.*)

What is that?

MARIA. Is David—Mr. Abbott.

CURATE (*inspecting the bathroom door through his pince-nez*). Oh, I see he is engaged. I had better return at a more convenient moment. (*He turns to go and then turns back.*) Why is he beating upon the door in that unaccountable way?

MARIA. 'E cannot get out.

CURATE. Oh really? Extraordinary. You haven't locked him in, I suppose?

MARIA. No. The door 'e is stuck.

CURATE. Tut, tut. Most unfortunate. May I? (*He tries the handle gingerly.*) Yes, it is, isn't it? (*Loudly.*) Can you hear me, Mr. Abbott?

   (*He starts away as there is a spate of renewed banging and hoarse shouts of undetermined origin.*)

Courage, my son. Succour is nigh! (*He retreats some distance, removes his clerical hat and pince-nez and gropes round short-sightedly for the door.*) Perhaps you would point me in the right direction.

MARIA. Don't you think it would be best not to—

CURATE. Now you must leave this to me.

   (MARIA *"sights" him towards the bathroom.*)

Fortescue to the rescue!

   (*He rushes headlong at the bathroom door, which opens at the critical moment, and he disappears inside in a flurry of steam. There is a loud splash.* MRS. BOTTLE *comes staggering out, her cap and tools abandoned and her hair awry. She hastily bangs the door tight and locks it, then sinks on to the couch and shuts her eyes. After a moment the handle is rattled and the banging begins again.*)

CURATE (*off*). Help, help. Dear lady, deliverance!

MARIA. Do you think we should?

MRS. BOTTLE. Not likely. 'E ain't got no clothes on.

CURATE (*off*). Come, come, madam. Will you kindly extricate me from this ridiculous— What? Go away. No! No! Will you let go, sir. Help! Help!

   (*This is followed by another splash and further incoherent cries.*)

MARIA. What are they doing? (*She goes to the sideboard and pours a drink.*)

MRS. BOTTLE. Mixed bathing by the sound of it. 'Oo! I've come over all unnecessary! (*She mops her brow with a big red spotted hanky.*) You 'aven't got a drop of something 'andy, I suppose, to soothe me feelings?

(MARIA *hands her a glass of rhubarb and dandelion.*)

MARIA. Try some of Auntie's special.

(MRS. BOTTLE *dabs some behind each ear and drains the glass. She coughs appreciatively and wipes her mouth with her sleeve.*)

MRS. BOTTLE. That's a bit of all right.

(*There are strange noises from the bathroom and* MARIA *looks apprehensive.*)

Oh, take no notice. They'll settle down in a bit. 'Ere, wot did you want to go and shove me in there for?

MARIA. I am sorry, but I was not knowing David was in there.

MRS. BOTTLE. You orter know when yer 'usband's' aving a bath. It's an annual event with Mr. Bottle.

MARIA. Oh, but we are not married, you see.

MRS. BOTTLE. Hmph! Fine state of affairs, I must say! I dunno wot Mr. Bottle's going to say, straight I don't. 'E's very partic'lar about the 'ouses 'e visits. "Always make sure you get a nice clean joint!" 'e says—

(*The door-bell rings.*)

'Allo. More fun and games!

(MARIA *opens the door to reveal* MRS. SCOTT, *still carrying the sandwiches, and* MRS. MACWHIMBLE, *who glares sourly at* MARIA *and* MRS. BOTTLE.)

MRS. SCOTT. Thank you, dear. I didn't take a key.

(*She advances to* C. *and notices* MRS. BOTTLE.)

Oh! How do you do. Have a water-cress sandwich.

MRS. BOTTLE. Don't mind if I do.

(*She takes one.* MARIA *refuses.*)

MARIA. Is Mrs. Bottle. She is looking for trouble in the bathroom.

MRS. BOTTLE. And I found more nor I bargained for!

MRS. MAC (*coming forward* R. *of* MRS. SCOTT). Are you criticizing my bathroom?

MRS. BOTTLE. There ain't nothing wrong with the bathroom, ducks, except it wasn't really built to 'old parties in.

MRS. SCOTT. What do you mean?

MRS. BOTTLE (*airily waving her sandwich*). Well, listen for yerself.

(*They listen, but all is quiet.*)

MRS. MAC. I can't 'ear nothing. (*She sniffs.*) You been drinking? Disgusting!

(MRS. BOTTLE *rises and comes* L. *of* MRS. SCOTT.)

MRS. BOTTLE. You'd have 'ad a nip, too, if you'd been through wot I 'ave. (*She lowers her voice to a dramatic and hoarse whisper.*) There's something gharstly in there!

(*She points at the bathroom and, as they all look, helps herself to another sandwich.*)

MRS. MAC (*snorting*). Hmph! 'Allucinations!

MRS. BOTTLE. Well, I never 'eard it called that before. Look for yerself if you don't believe me. Only don't say I didn't warn yer. 'Orrible it is!

(*She subsides on to the couch and takes a bite at her sandwich.* MRS. MACWHIMBLE *seizes an umbrella from the stand and advances towards the door. She unlocks it and she and* MRS. SCOTT *stand well back.*)

MRS. MAC. Come out, whatever you are.

(*The door slowly opens a crack and a bare arm comes stealthily out. Its owner remains hidden. The arm, after groping round in a futile and helpless way, discovers the pile of* MARIA'S *underclothes, grabs them and disappears. The door closes with a bang. This is followed by a cry of horror from within. The ladies have watched this phenomenon in awestruck silence. They all jump as the door slams.*)

Well, 'oo would 'ave believed it?

MRS. SCOTT. Isn't it exciting!

MARIA. 'E 'as taken my clothes!

MRS. BOTTLE (*reclining on the couch*). You ain't seen nothing. That was only a trailer. I seen the full-length feature! Gharstly! The Monkey's Paw ain't nothing to it. (*She shudders with grim satisfaction.*)

MRS. MAC. Well, I don't care if it's the Loch Ness monster. 'E ain't living in my bath rent free! (*She hammers on the door.*) Do you 'ear me! Come out and face me like a man!

MRS. BOTTLE. Strewth! You dunno wot you're asking!

(*The door-bell rings and* MRS. SCOTT *goes to answer it. She opens the door to reveal* DAVID *in clerical garb. He stands silent for a moment as they take him in.*)

DAVID (*gasping*). I got out of the window and down a drain-pipe.

MRS. SCOTT. Dear boy! You know you don't like heights.

(DAVID *staggers dramatically across the room and collapses into the easy-chair.*)

MARIA (*pointing to the bathroom*). Oh! Then what about—?

But she gets no further. There is a loud explosion from within and the door is blown off its hinges. Out staggers the CURATE *surrounded by a good deal of smoke and steam. His face is blackened and he is indecorously clad in combinations,* MARIA'S *pants and bra and* MRS. BOTTLE'S *cloth cap. He stands in misery as*

THE CURTAIN SLOWLY FALLS

ACT THREE

The late afternoon of the same day. The scene is unchanged except that the table has been cleared, the water-cress sandwiches have been relegated to the sideboard and the room generally looks tidier than it did at the end of Act Two. DAVID's pyjamas and dressing-gown have gone and the bathroom door is back in place.

KATE is discovered curled up on the couch making a telephone call.

KATE. Yes, the curate, poor man. He kept shaking his fist at David and piping about an affront to his cloth. Anyway, we calmed him down in the end and mopped up the froth—froth, dear, with a cloth—no, not the curate's cloth, the cloor floth, oh damn! Well, anyway, we wrapped him up in a blanket and the others have taken him home in the car with a pile of water-cress sandwiches to keep his strength up— (*The door-bell rings.*) Oh, that must be them now. I must fly. Tea on Wednesday?—'Bye now. (*She puts down the receiver, pats her hair into place in front of the mirror and opens the front door. A POSTMAN enters, holding out a package and a flimsy.*)

POSTMAN. Registered parcel, mum. Sign 'ere please.

KATE. Oh, thank you. My, it's heavy! Have you got a pencil?

POSTMAN. No, sorry.

KATE. I thought you people always carried one, very blunt and black.

POSTMAN. I lorst it.

KATE. Never mind. I'll find one.

(*She comes back into the room and starts to rummage about in the dresser drawer. The POSTMAN follows her in, closing the door behind him and drops his very empty sack on the floor. Now we can see him clearly there is something oddly familiar about the face under the peak cap and the more observant will spot that it is, in fact, the TAXIMAN-BURGLAR in yet another role and heavily disguised under a drooping moustache which does nothing for him. While KATE seeks and eventually locates a pencil, he looks anxiously all round the room and even stoops down and looks under the sideboard. KATE watches him in some surprise, shrugs, signs the slip and hands it back.*)

Thank you. Did you drop something?

BURGLAR. Thank you, miss. You 'aven't, I suppose, come across a small parcel—about so big? I lorst one 'ereabouts yusterday.

KATE. You are losing things. No, I'm afraid I haven't.

BURGLAR. Mind if I 'ave a shufty—er—look round?

KATE. Well, it is a little inconvenient, as it happens.

BURGLAR. Oh, come on, lady, be a sport. It's a serious matter when a postman loses his packets. It's like—well—

KATE. Foolish virgins?

BURGLAR. I knew you'd understand.

KATE. Oh, all right then, just for a minute.

  (*He crosses* L. *and peers behind the couch, then goes down on hands and knees and peers underneath it.* KATE *watches fascinated, shrugs and begins to unwrap the parcel.*)

You haven't tried under the carpet.

BURGLAR. That's an idea. (*He begins to burrow under the rug, then notices what she is doing.*) Oy! Don't do that!

  (*He jumps to his feet, but the paper is off by this time and inside is a house-brick.*)

KATE. Oh. This must be a joke.

BURGLAR (*crossing to* KATE). You didn't orter 'ave opened that parcel.

KATE. But why not?

BURGLAR. 'Cos it's addressed to Mister Abbott. I didn't think you'd open it.

KATE. But why should anyone send David a brick—and register it, too?

BURGLAR. I daresay it's a sample from a building society. Give away anything nowadays.

KATE. Come to think of it, this is a funny time of day to deliver parcels—and you're not our usual postman, are you? (*She moves towards the door.*) I think you'd better go.

BURGLAR. I wouldn't go near that door, lady.

KATE. Why not?

BURGLAR. Because I been losing things all day and I might lose me temper. (*He draws a revolver.*) Then this might go off.

KATE. Oh! (*She almost screams, then recovers her composure.*) And what exactly are you after?

BURGLAR. I've told yer. I'm looking for a small packet I dropped last time I was 'ere.

KATE. Oh, so you were here last night. I'm so glad—David was telling the truth after all.

BURGLAR. You might be glad, but I shan't forget it in a 'urry. Creepin' about all hours like a week-end at Brighton. And in all the curfuffle blow me if I didn't drop me necklace.

KATE. Necklace?

BURGLAR. Er—yus.

KATE. Perhaps the fastener was loose.

BURGLAR. Eh? No, I collect 'em. You 'aven't seen it, I suppose?

KATE (*coolly, walking* D.L. *and sitting in the easy chair*). I'm afraid you're too late. We handed it over to the police this morning. I'm expecting them round any time now for more details.

BURGLAR. I'd best be off, then. (*He moves towards the door, but is stopped short by the bell.* KATE *jumps to her feet.*) 'Ere, where can I 'ide?

KATE. Get into your sack. (*She puts the brick down on the chair.*)

BURGLAR (*just stopping himself in time*). Lady, this ain't no joking matter. Me reputation's at stake. (*He looks round wildly and points at the bedroom door.*) Wot's in there?

KATE. The bedroom.

BURGLAR. Well, this ain't the time to be shy. You answer the door and get rid of 'em quick. And don't forget, I'll be in 'ere wiv me little persuader (*He waves his revolver dramatically and gets it tangled up in his sack which he has picked up.*)—listening in to every word. (*He disappears into the bedroom and* KATE, *somewhat apprehensively, opens the door to disclose* CELLINI. *He appears as in Act Two, except that he is not wearing an overcoat. He is still wearing his silk scarf.*)

KATE. Oh!

CELLINI (*doffing his hat*). Good afternoon. Mrs. Abbott?

KATE. Yes, but I— (*She looks desperately at the bedroom door, then raises her voice.*) Good afternoon, Inspector; do come in.

CELLINI (*crossing to* C., *bewildered*). Ah, there is a mistake. I am—

KATE. No, no! You've come about the necklace. (*She closes the door.*)

CELLINI. Ze necklace! (*He takes her by the shoulders.*) You know about ze necklace?

KATE (*alarmed*). No! I mean yes! Oh!

CELLINI (*menacingly*). What do you know?

KATE. N-nothing. I—I— (*Whispers.*) There's a man in the bedroom with a little persuader. (*She points, then aloud.*) I'm so glad you came round, Inspector.

CELLINI. *Basta!* What is zis Inspector?

KATE (*whispers*). In the bedroom! He's got a gun.

CELLINI. So. (*He strides to the bedroom.*)

KATE (*screams*). No! Look out! He'll shoot!

> (*She dives behind the couch as* CELLINI *throws the door open and bursts in. Nothing happens and after a moment he returns and looks round in some surprise.* KATE's *head slowly appears over the back of the couch.*)

(*Gulping.*) Nobody?

CELLINI. Nobody! You are sure 'e—

KATE. Yes, yes. He threatened me with a gun. It was a burglar.

CELLINI. Well 'e 'as burgled off. Now what is zis about a necklace?

KATE. Oh, thank you.

> (*She runs over and hugs him in relief. He is a little taken aback,*

but pats her comfortingly on the shoulder. At this moment the front door opens and DAVID *enters.*)

DAVID. Katie, darling, guess what— Oh, I beg your pardon. (*He turns to go out again, but stops short and charges back.*) Here, I say, that's mine.

KATE (*releasing herself and restoring her self-composure as she advances to meet him*). Oh, David, there you are. I'm so glad you've come.

DAVID (*advancing aggressively*). Oh, like that, is it? Now look here, you— (*He makes a fist at* CELLINI, *who shakes it amiably.*)

CELLINI. 'Ow do you do. I am Cellini.

DAVID. Pleased to meet you. Now what the devil are you doing with my wife?

CELLINI (*loudly and firmly*). Carlo Cellini—Maria 'as mention me yes?

KATE. Who?

DAVID. What? You don't mean you're Maria's fancy?

CELLINI. *Si.* We are engaged.

KATE (*jumping up*). Her fiancé!

DAVID. Oh Lord! But you can't be. You're too old—I mean you're in Italy.

CELLINI (*spreads his hands in mock apology*). Maria did not tell you I come? She telephone me and say she is ina trouble. So I come to 'elp.

DAVID. Help!

KATE (*recovering her composure and becoming the hostess*). Won't you sit down, Mr. Cellini? Here, let me take your hat.

(*She pushes the hat and stick into* DAVID'S *hands and escorts* CELLINI *to the couch, where he sits.*)

You must forgive us. We had no idea you were coming. Maria should have told us. You must think us very inhospitable. David, a drink.

DAVID. Yes, please. Oh, I see what you mean.

(*She pushes* DAVID *towards the sideboard. He lays the hat and stick on the chair by the bathroom and proceeds to pour two drinks.*)

CELLINI. Ah, Mrs. Abbott, I am quite understanding. Please say no more.

DAVID (*casually*). Did Maria—er—Miss Lauro say just what sort of trouble she is in?

CELLINI. *Si.* Is a man 'oo is worrying her.

KATE. Hmph!

DAVID. Oh Lord! (*He seizes a cigar-box off the sideboard.*) Have a cigar —er— (*The cigar-box is full of buttons which cascade into* CELLINI'S *lap.* DAVID *pulls out a roll of peppermints from his pocket.*) Have a peppermint. The hint with the mole!

CELLINI (*has by this time taken out his own opulent cigar-case and offers one to* DAVID). Thank you, no. 'Ave one of mine.

DAVID. Oh, thank you.

> (*He takes one and is about to strike a match, only to find* CELLINI *has already produced an ornate lighter with which he lights* DAVID'S *cigar and his own.*)

Thanks! (DAVID *hands* CELLINI *his drink and collects a refill for himself. Then he settles down in the arm-chair to enjoy his cigar.*) Ahhh! Ow! (*He jumps up again and reveals that he has sat on the brick.*) Hallo, the place is falling to bits.

CELLINI (*sips his drink and shudders violently*). Agh!—Is good. Where is Maria?

KATE. She went out with Mother and David. They had to take a curate home. What's become of them, David? I thought they were coming back with you.

DAVID. Mother's driving round and round the block trying to find somewhere to park. (*The front door-bell rings and* KATE *opens it. Enter* MARIA.) Oh, there you are. We were beginning to think you'd migrated.

> (KATE *leaves the door ajar while* MARIA *crosses to* C.)

MARIA. 'Allo, David. We couldn't find anywhere to park and—Oh! (*She has caught sight of* CELLINI, *who has risen and stubbed out his cigar.*)

DAVID. Surprise, surprise. All the way from sunny Italy.

KATE. Isn't it wonderful. (*She crosses to* DAVID.) You should have told us he was coming.

> (MARIA *stands nonplussed.*)

CELLINI (*advancing towards her*). 'Allo, darling.

> (MARIA, *still puzzled, makes no response.*)

DAVID. Don't mind us. Go ahead—kiss her.

CELLINI. *Carissima!* (*He kisses her.*)

MARIA. 'Ow dare you, you dirty olda man! (*She slaps his face and he restrains an impulse to slap back, then bows.*)

DAVID (*to* KATE). I read a story once called "Latins are Lousy Lovers", but this is ridiculous.

KATE. Well, I must say it's a funny way to greet your fiancé.

MARIA (*astounded*). My fiancé!

CELLINI (*quickly, holding her firmly round the waist*). But, of course, *mia carissima.* Don't say you've changed your mind. (*He makes warning faces at her as she struggles to get free.*)

MARIA (*whispers*). You are mad! (*Aloud.*) 'Carlo darling, how nice of you to come.

CELLINI. 'Ow could I stay away from my treasure.

MARIA. 'Ow indeed! (*Still wriggling to escape.*)

> (KATE *and* DAVID *have been standing together with their heads on one side and a soppy look on their faces watching all this.* MRS. SCOTT *enters through the open door and* MARIA *breaks free.*)

MRS. SCOTT (*to* C.). There, that's done. I found just the place for the car. I left it in a taxi rank with a glove over the driving mirror. (*To* CELLINI.) Oh, good afternoon. Do introduce us, Maria.

(*But* MARIA *has warily retired* D.R. *and is keeping as far away from* CELLINI *as possible.*)

CELLINI (*concealing his annoyance at the interruption*). Carlo Cellini. (*He takes her hand, kisses it, gives a formal bow and clicks his heels.*)

MRS. SCOTT. Oh, how delightfully old-fashioned. (*She curtsies.*) *Enchanté, M'sieur.* I'm Mrs. Scott. You know Maria, of course.

DAVID. He's her fancy—fiancé.

MRS. SCOTT. Ah, my dear boy, how delightful. Maria, come here, you wicked girl. You never told us he was coming. I thought you looked a little pink when I came in. Been making up for lost time, eh?

CELLINI (*charm oozing out of every pore*). You musta be Mrs. Abbott's sister.

(KATE *is none too pleased about this, but* MRS. SCOTT *is delighted.*)

MRS. SCOTT. Ah! you wicked man. Don't try any of that Italian charm on me; I'm much too old. (*She sits on the couch and pats the seat beside her.*) Now come and tell me all about Rome.

KATE. Mother dear, don't you think we ought to let Mr. Cellini settle down first? He's only just arrived.

MRS. SCOTT (*springing up again*). Yes, yes, of course. What am I thinking about? Quite carried away. Do forgive me, Mr.—er— (*She holds up her hand to be kissed again.*)

CELLINI (*bowing again*). Cellini.

MRS. SCOTT. Yes. Well, you and Maria have a cosy chat while we all go and tidy up outside. Come along, children. (*She goes into kitchen.*)

KATE. Come on, David. We'll do the dishes.

DAVID. Eh?

KATE. The dishes!

DAVID. But I wanted to ask him about—

KATE. Come on! (*She lugs him towards the kitchen.*) Can't you see they want to be alone?

MARIA (*panicking and trying, unsuccessfully, to escape past* CELLINI). No! Don't leave us alone! I mean there's no need for you to go, is there?

KATE (*archly*). I'm sure there's such a lot you have to say to one another.

CELLINI (*blandly*). *Si,* yes—there are one or two little matters to be settled.

(*He looks down affectionately at* MARIA, *who gulps and tries a shaky smile.* KATE *goes into kitchen.*)

DAVID (*standing grinning foolishly at the door*). Aha!

(KATE'S *arm reaches in, grabs his ear and extracts him. The kitchen door closes.* MARIA *sits at the table with her back to* CELLINI. *Suddenly he bends down to her from behind and his bland manner changes abruptly.*)

CELLINI (*venomously*). Well? Where is it? What 'ave you done with ze necklace?

MARIA. I tell you I don' 'ave it. Lasta night I wait and wait, but you don' come. So I put it under the pillow for safety and now look (*She crosses to the couch and lifts up the pillow.*)—see—is not there no more.

CELLINI. So, you makea ze fool of Cellini, eh? (*He puts his hands round her neck and forces her on to the couch. He lowers his voice almost to a caress.*) You know what 'appen to little girls 'oo try to double-cross Cellini? (*He massages her neck thoughtfully and squeezes a little harder.*) They get 'urt! (MARIA *struggles to escape, but he holds her down.*) And besides there is a little something you don' want people know about, eh?

MARIA. *Basta!* I 'ate you!

(*The kitchen door opens and* DAVID *enters. Immediately* CELLINI *turns his menacing position into a passionate embrace. All we can see of* MARIA *is a pair of threshing legs.*)

DAVID. Oh, I say, sorry to interrupt, but I must get a teacloth. We keep them in the bathroom—I don't know why. Promise I won't look. (*He crosses to the bathroom and they follow him with their eyes. At the door he turns slowly to meet their gaze.*) Er—having fun? Lots to talk about, eh?

CELLINI. But of course. We are making plans.

MARIA (*sotto voce*). *Porco!*

DAVID (*benevolently*). Ah, young love! (*He looks hard at* CELLINI'S *bald spot.*) Well, love anyway. (*A thought strikes him.*) *Porco?* I say, doesn't that mean pig? I'm learning Italian, you know.

CELLINI. *Si*, is a term of endearment.

DAVID. Good show. I must remember that. Now, what is it the French call one another?

CELLINI. Teacloth!

DAVID. Eh? I haven't heard that one.

CELLINI. You came to fetch a teacloth.

DAVID. Did I? Oh, yes. Well, if you're quite sure there's nothing you want.

CELLINI. I wanta one thing only and Maria 'as that, 'aven't you, *carissima?*

DAVID. Ahem! Quite! Well—er—make yourselves at home. (*He dives into the bathroom, reappears with a tea-towel and, using it as a screen, dashes for the kitchen.*)

MARIA. David!

    (She rises and makes a desperate effort to move towards him, but is restrained by CELLINI.*)*

DAVID *(turning eagerly)*. Yes?

CELLINI *(menacingly)*. Yes?

MARIA *(after a moment's hesitation)*. Good-bye!

DAVID. What? Oh, good-bye! *(He comes across and shakes hands with her and* CELLINI, *then goes into the kitchen, scratching his head in bewilderment.)*

CELLINI. Now, little fool! *(He pounces at her.)*

MARIA. Keep away. *(She backs away and looks round desperately for a weapon, finally picking up a feather duster which is lying on the sideboard. She beats him over the head.)*

CELLINI *(shakes her)*. Where is it? Where is it?

    (Suddenly the kitchen door opens again and MRS. SCOTT *sweeps in. Swiftly they transform again into a cosy huddle.)*

MRS. SCOTT. You're the very man I want. *(*CELLINI *looks alarmed as she descends on him.)* I've got my eye on a delightful little piece of pottery in a shop near here. The dealer says it's seventeenth-century Italian and I want you to come along and give me your expert opinion.

CELLINI *(spreading his hands)*. Alas, dear lady, I am sorry, but I am knowing nothing about ze antiques.

MRS. SCOTT. Oh, nonsense! Don't be modest. All you Italians are terribly artistic. Isn't that right, Maria?

    *(*MARIA *has taken refuge behind the table.)*

MARIA. *Si!* Is right. 'E love old valuables.

MRS. SCOTT. Well, there you are, you see. Besides, look at Picasso.

CELLINI. But 'e come from Spain.

MRS. SCOTT. That's got nothing to do with it. Come along. *(She takes his arm and steers him towards the door.)*

CELLINI. I am sorry, but I cannot—

MRS. SCOTT *(handing him his hat and stick)*. There's your little stick. Now I won't take no for an answer. It's only just round the corner. I'm sure Maria can spare you for a few minutes; she won't run away, will you, dear? *(She hustles* CELLINI *out of the door, but he forces his way back in again.)*

CELLINI. She 'ad better not!

MRS. SCOTT. Come along then. *(To* MARIA.*)* Tell Kate we shan't be long. *(She pushes* CELLINI *to the door, where he bows her out first and takes the opportunity to deliver a parting shot.)*

CELLINI. I come back!

MRS. SCOTT *(reaching in and dragging him out)*. Do tell me, Mr. Bellini, don't you agree the frescoes at Florence are— *(They go off together.)*

CELLINI *(off)*. The name is Cellini, madam—

(MARIA *at once shows signs of panic. She throws the feather duster on to a chair and rushes into the bedroom. She reappears with one of her suitcases and an armful of clothes which she begins to throw into the case, muttering to herself.*)

MARIA. Oh I cannot go in zis!

(*She unzips her dress, throws it into the case and marches into the bedroom in her bra and panties. The door closes after her. This is the signal for* DAVID *to appear; he looks all round, then calls back into the kitchen.*)

DAVID. It's all right. They must have gone out.

(*He enters, followed by* KATE, *who is carrying a basket and putting on her coat.* DAVID *suddenly notices the open suitcase.*)

Hallo, hallo, what's all this? Signs of departure?

KATE. Well, you didn't expect them to stay for ever, did you?

DAVID. But they've only just come.

KATE. I'm going round to the grocer's to get them something for the journey.

DAVID (*picking up the plate of decrepit water-cress sandwiches*). How about these?

KATE. I don't think so. I shan't be long. (*She pauses at the door.*) I suppose it's safe to leave you alone for five minutes?

DAVID. Good Lord, woman, anyone would think we were living in the wilds. Whatever do you think is going to happen to me?

KATE. I can't imagine, but whatever it is, I shan't believe you!

(KATE *leaves, complete with shopping-basket, and* DAVID *settles down with a paper and a water-cress sandwich in the easy-chair with his back to the bedroom door.*)

DAVID (*chuckling*). Poor old Katie!

(MARIA *re-enters from the bedroom, wearing a blouse and panties. She deposits more clothes in the case and returns to the bedroom oblivious of* DAVID. *She shuts the door with a bang.* DAVID *jumps and looks straight ahead wide-eyed. He gulps and peers over the chair. All is quiet. He shrugs and returns to his paper.* MARIA *enters dressed as before. This time she sees* DAVID *and comes to stand behind his chair, thus concealing her lower half. In this position she appears positively decent.*)

MARIA. Oh, David, there you are.

DAVID (*leaps three feet into the air from a sitting start and gives a strangled scream*). Ahh! (*He covers his head with the paper and peers out from under.*) Oh, it's you!

MARIA. David, you must 'elp me get ready.

DAVID. I thought you'd gone out. (*He stands up and catches sight of* MARIA's *lower half. He turns his back, putting his hand over his eyes.*) Oh my hat! (*He takes another peep and returns to hiding.*) Haven't you forgotten something?

C.O.F.—E

MARIA (*peering into her case, her back to the audience*). I don' think so. I am travelling light.

DAVID. You're telling me!

MARIA. Please, David, you must 'elp me. I am in terrible trouble.

DAVID (*taking a look*). So am I!

MARIA (*bending over the case again*). You don' appreciate my position!

DAVID (*looks again and raises an eyebrow at the audience*). Oh, I don't know!

MARIA. I 'ave no one to turn to.

DAVID. Without wishing to seem indelicate—what about your boy-friend?

MARIA. Carlo? Oh, 'im! 'E is gone off to look at some olda piece of china.

DAVID. And left you like this! He must be keen on geography. Don't you think you ought to put something else on?

MARIA. You don' understand. He is coming back soon and so I must be ready first.

DAVID. I say, steady on!

(MARIA *goes to the bedroom door and beckons him.*)

MARIA. You come and 'elp me get ready, eh?

(*She goes into bedroom.* DAVID *runs his finger round his collar.*)

DAVID. Another old Italian custom, I suppose. Oh well, duty to one's guests!

(*He begins to roll up his sleeves and as the idea grows on him he rubs his hands together, leaps into the air growling furiously, and clambers over the couch towards the bedroom. He stops short, returns to the sideboard for the bottle of brandy, adjusts his tie and walks expectantly into the bedroom, closing the door behind him. A moment later there is the sound of a slap and* MARIA *reappears, now fully dressed, carrying a second suitcase.* DAVID *follows her out, ruefully rubbing his cheek.*)

O.K. So I'm sorry! How was I to know you meant help you to pack?

MARIA. You men are all ze same. Now I go before he come back. (*She picks up the other suitcase and starts to lug them both to the door. One bursts open and tips the contents on to the floor.*) Oh! (*She kicks the case once or twice while* DAVID *starts to stuff everything back in again.*) It 'as all gone wrong!

DAVID. Yes, yes. You'd better sit down and have a drink. It'll help you to calm down. Now just you relax and tell Uncle David all about it. (*He shuts the case and puts both cases by the front door.*)

MARIA (*sighing and sitting on the couch*). All right. I suppose you find out sometime, so I make a bare breast of things.

DAVID. Good show! (*He busies himself pouring drinks.*)

MARIA. Cellini—'e is not Carlo.

DAVID. Oh, I see! (*He couldn't be more puzzled.*)

MARIA. 'E is Cellini—Arturo Cellini, and 'e know my father.

DAVID. How nice! You mean he isn't your fiancé? (*He hands her a drink and sits beside her.*)

MARIA. What, that olda man! No, Carlo is young and 'andsome—and 'e must not find out why I am 'ere.

DAVID. Well, if it's not a silly question, why are you here?

MARIA. Is difficult to explain. My father, 'e is a, 'ow you say—an old leg.

DAVID. A what? Oh, you mean an old lag—an ex-convict?

MARIA. *Si*, yes—a jail-fowl. Well, this Cellini write and say if I don' do what 'e want he will tell Carlo about my father.

DAVID. But that's blackmail! What did he want you to do?

MARIA. Get something in past the customs man.

DAVID. Smuggling, eh? What was it—brandy?

MARIA. Diamonds.

DAVID. Diamonds! (*He jumps to his feet and drains his glass to steady himself.*)

MARIA. *Si.* A necklace. (*She jumps to her feet in agitation.*) But now somebody steal it and Cellini think I am double-crossing him.

DAVID. It's about time somebody told this Cellini fellow where he gets off.

MARIA. Oh, David. Would you really?

DAVID. Me? Hey, wait a minute.

MARIA (*throws her arms round him and kisses him in relief*). You are verree sweet.

DAVID. Yes, but look here.

MARIA. But you must be careful. 'E is armed.

DAVID (*aghast*). Armed!

MARIA. Always 'e carry a stick.

DAVID (*relieved*). Oh, is that all.

MARIA. A sword-stick.

DAVID (*now highly alarmed*). Eh?

MARIA. But you are not afraid of 'im?

DAVID. Afraid? Who me? Ha ha! (*He makes one or two deft sword strokes, receives an imaginary thrust in the tummy and collapses into the chair.*)

MARIA (*perching on the arm of his chair*). Oh, David, I feel so different now you are going to 'elp me. I don' want to run away now.

DAVID. I do!

MARIA. I am so glad I tell you everything. Otherwise I should not 'ave known 'ow brave you are.

DAVID. Neither should I!

MARIA. 'E will be back soon. You will not 'urt 'im much?

DAVID. Not if I can get away in time. (*A pause.*) I say, Maria?
MARIA. Yes, David?
DAVID (*nonchalantly*). I suppose they don't fight duels in Italy nowadays?
MARIA. No, only in Sicily.
>   (DAVID *sighs with relief.*)
Cellini come from Sicily.
>   (DAVID *reacts with horror.*)
Is something wrong?
DAVID. No! Oh no! Just a bit out of practice at the old sword play, that's all.
MARIA. 'Ere, I show you. Is very easy. (*She crosses and takes up the umbrella from the stand.*) Come, stand up.
>   (*He does so, dejectedly.*)
Now then. 'E will come at you like so! (*She lunges at him with the umbrella.*)
DAVID. Here, I say, watch out!
MARIA. And you must feint.
DAVID. Don't worry. I'll be out cold.
MARIA. No, no. Like zis. (*She picks up the feather duster and hands it to him. On second thoughts he swops this for the umbrella.*) Now, you attack me.
>   (DAVID *wags the umbrella about vaguely.*)
No, properly!
>   (*He makes a desperate lunge which* MARIA *calmly parries with the duster and* DAVID *finishes up in a heap on the couch.*)
You see. Is simple.
DAVID (*picking himself up*). Oh that's just great.
MARIA. Now I attack you. (*She lunges at him and they fight a splendid running battle round the couch.*)
DAVID. Have at you!—Ha!—Mind the lamp!—Yield, yield!—Oops! (*As he trips over the carpet and finishes up on the couch again.*) Did I win? (*He climbs to his feet.*)
MARIA. No, David. You are not 'olding it right. 'Ere, I show you. You see, like zis. One 'and 'ere, the other like so.
>   (*They get into a suitable huddle and* DAVID *becomes aware of her closeness. The demonstration becomes a dangerous cuddle.*)
DAVID (*softly*). Maria?
MARIA (*almost a whisper*). Si?
DAVID. Wouldn't it be as well if the door-bell rang?
MARIA. I am thinking maybe yes.
>   (*The door-bell obliges and* DAVID *and* MARIA *spring apart.*)
'Is 'im!
>   (DAVID *runs behind the couch and leaves the umbrella there.*)
David! You promised!

DAVID. Just taking up a strategic position.
MARIA. You wish I should open the door?
DAVID. Not half! I mean no! Stand back!
　　　(*He picks up the feather duster and strikes a heroic attitude with it poised aloft. Gingerly he edges across the room and is just stretching his hand out for the door-knob when the bell rings again. He turns to run and bumps into* MARIA, *who pushes him back to the door, opens it from under his arm and leaves him to face the consequences. He shuts his eyes and retreats behind the door as it swings open to reveal* MRS. MACWHIMBLE. *His outstretched feather duster tickles her under the nose and she pushes the "weapon" aside scornfully and stands, arms folded, watching his antics. He opens one eye, jumps and scrambles to safety with a shout.*)
Ow! Hallo, Mrs. MacTremble. I'm all of a whimble. I mean I thought you were a smuggler. I—er—I was just doing a spot of dusting. (*He flicks a speck of dust off her shoulder.*)
MRS. MAC. Sorry to disturb yer, I'm sure. I come to give you this. (*She holds out a piece of paper.*)
DAVID. Oh, how nice, thank you. What is it?
MRS. MAC. It's your formal written notice in writing to leave this 'ere desirable residence tomorrer.
DAVID. Oh!
MRS. MAC. On account of the sinful carryings-on as I've seen wiv me own eyes.
MARIA. That is not fair. David 'as done nothing.
MRS. MAC. Oh, you're still 'ere, are yer? I don't know 'ow you 'ave the bare-faced effrontery to stand there—
DAVID. You should have seen her just now.
MRS. MAC. I might 'ave known what to expect when I saw all them bottles.
DAVID. What, old Auntie's home-made! It wouldn't hurt a fly.
MRS. MAC (*darkly*). Alcohol is the devil's brew
　　　　　　　　And them what drinks it—
DAVID. Their nose turns blue. I tell you you're making a terrible mistake.
MRS. MAC. Oh, no, I ain't! I know what you are with yer 'ome-made ginger beer and yer gramyphone—beatniks, that's what! And now you can beat it! (*She dives her hand into her apron pocket and pulls out a small package.*) And you can take this with you. I found it in the 'all. Mary Joanna I shouldn't wonder. (*She throws the package at* DAVID *and leaves with a final snort at* MARIA.)
DAVID. And good luck to you, too! Silly old beezum! (*He opens the packet and extracts the necklace.*)
MARIA (*rushing forward*). *Eccola!* That is it. Ze necklace! (*She tears

it away from him and holds it up.) Thank goodness, is come back. Now we 'ave nothing to worry about. (*She moves* D.L., *admiring the necklace.*)

DAVID. But dash it all, Maria, you're not the right shape to be a smuggler. They're supposed to have wooden legs and whiskers. You're too nice!

MARIA. Ah, David. You are very nice also. (*She kisses him on the cheek.*) But you enjoy the smuggler's brandy, yes?

DAVID. Yes, but that's different. Anyway, I won't let you do it.

(MARIA *has turned her back on* DAVID *and as he speaks he creeps up on her and suddenly snatches the necklace away. He holds it high up out of her reach.*)

MARIA. *Ladro!* 'Oo is the thief now? Give it to me, David.

(*She stretches up, but can't quite reach.*)

Please, David. I ask you nicely.

DAVID. It's for your own good. I'm protecting you against yourself.

(MARIA *picks up a vase and advances on him.*)

MARIA. Give—it—to—me!

DAVID. Now, Maria. (*Backing up.*) Now, don't be silly. That vase is very valuable.

(*He falls back on to the couch and* MARIA *pins him down with the vase upraised. At this moment* CELLINI *enters through the front door.*)

CELLINI. Aha! (*He places his hat on the umbrella stand.*)

MARIA. *Madre mia!*

DAVID.. Oops!

(*They climb rather awkwardly off the sofa and* DAVID *snatches the vase from* MARIA *and hides the necklace inside.*)

CELLINI (*coming to* C.). So, Mistaire Abbott! You attack my fiancé, eh?

DAVID. Dash it, she was trying to dot me one with a vase! (*He is hiding the vase behind him.*) Anyway, you're a fine one to talk. I know what you're up to. (*He manages to shuffle the vase on to the sideboard unseen by* CELLINI.) And if you're not out of this house in ten seconds I'll— I'll call the police!

MARIA. Be careful, David!

DAVID. I'm not afraid of him and his sword-stick. I've had lessons.

(*He seizes the umbrella and flourishes it as* CELLINI *advances.*)

En garde!

CELLINI (*putting his stick aside and taking out a revolver*). Touché!

MARIA (*screams*). Look out, David!

DAVID (*throwing his weapon on to the couch*). That's not fair. You're supposed to use your stick.

CELLINI. Ah, that Maria, she is incurably romantic. Now enough of zis playing. I want ze necklace.

DAVID. Say please.

CELLINI (*bowing*). I would like ze necklace, please.

DAVID. Well, you're damned well not getting it.

CELLINI. Mr. Abbott, you are forgetting. (*He taps the gun.*) I am a very
good shot and your ears stick out.

          (DAVID *claps his hands to his ears.*)

Maria, you will give it to me now! Already I 'ave waste too much
time on a wild duck chase.

DAVID. A what?

CELLINI. A wild duck chase. Your mother-in-law is a difficult woman
to escape. Now, you will stand over there with your face to the wall
—please, Mr. Abbott.

      (*After some hesitation,* DAVID *moves down to face the wall* D.R.)

DAVID. Are we going to play creepy-mouse?

CELLINI. Be quiet! Please. (*To* MARIA.) Tie 'is 'ands.

DAVID. Don't be silly, old chap.

CELLINI. Quick.

MARIA. But there is no rope.

CELLINI. Tear up one of those sheets. (*Pointing to the couch.*)

DAVID (*turning round in agitation*). No, no! Kate'll have kittens. Those
are her second-best sheets.

CELLINI (*helping* MARIA *to tear them*). Were, Mr. Abbott, were, were.

DAVID. And whir, whir to you, too! You sound like a bee in a bottle.

      (MARIA *ties his hands behind him.* CELLINI *lights a cigarette,*
keeping a wary eye on them.)

MARIA. David, I am sorry. I bring you ze big trouble.

CELLINI. Tight knots, if you please. I test them.

DAVID. Ow! Steady on. Leave us a bit of circulation. You won't get
away with this, Cellini.

CELLINI. So? We see, eh? (*He tests the knots.*) Good. I compliment
you on your knots.

DAVID. That's what comes of being a Girl Guide.

CELLINI. Well, I was a Boy Scout. (*To* MARIA.) Face ze wall wiz your
'ands be'ind you.

MARIA. Oh, David!

      (CELLINI *lays down his gun and starts to tie up* MARIA.)

DAVID. Pecker up, lass. It could be worse. He might have been wearing his Boy Scout trousers. Bo!

      (*He makes a move as if to jump on* CELLINI, *who swiftly picks up*
his gun. DAVID *contents himself with pulling a face at him.*)

CELLINI. Nothing foolish, Mr. Abbott. All right, you may turn round
now.

DAVID. Thank goodness for that. This wallpaper's hideous.

CELLINI. Now, Maria! You would not like Mr. Abbott to get 'urt,
eh? So you tell me where ze necklace is 'idden.

(*He brings the lighted end of his cigarette near* DAVID's *face.*
DAVID *goes cross-eyed looking at it and bursts out coughing.*)
You are not supposed to do zat. You 'ave blown ze end right off!

DAVID. I'm most frightfully sorry, but you really ought to try filter
tipped.

(CELLINI *lights his cigarette again.*)

CELLINI. Well, Maria—I am impatient.

MARIA. What shall I do, David?

DAVID. Don't you say a word, old girl. He's bluffing.

CELLINI (*casually burning* DAVID's *hand*). I think not.

DAVID. Ow! Well, go on—tell him! Tell him!

MARIA. No, David! Stop it, stop it! I tell you. It is—

(*The door-bell cuts her short and* CELLINI *turns angrily.*)

DAVID (*singing*). Thank heavens for little bells!

CELLINI. Quick, in there!

(*He hustles them towards the bathroom.*)

DAVID. Oh no! Not again! I'm allergic to bath salts.

MARIA. Are you 'urt, David?

DAVID. Touch of cramp in the benevolence, that's all. Are you any
good at screaming? Oof!

(CELLINI *pushes their heads together and ties his silk scarf round
their faces as a gag. He then bundles them crab-wise into the bathroom and locks the door. Putting his gun into his pocket, he opens
the front door and reveals* KATE *carrying a basket of shopping.*)

KATE. Oh, Mr. Cellini, thank you. I couldn't get at my key. (*She
enters and dumps the basket on the table.*) Where's David?

CELLINI. 'E is—er—taking a bath.

KATE. Taking a bath! But he had one this morning! (*She crosses
towards the bathroom.*)

CELLINI (*spreading his hands*). Well, is a 'ot day. Now, Mrs. Abbott,
if you will excuse me—

KATE. Won't you and Maria have a meal before you go? Where is
she, by the way?

CELLINI. Who, Maria? Oh, she's not far off. I arrange to meet 'er in
the basin—I mean at ze station. You *scusi*, eh? (*He bows and makes for
the door.*)

KATE (*to* C.). Well, yes, of course, but I feel I've been a very bad hostess.
And as for David— (*She looks fiercely at the bathroom.*) I'll have a few
words to say to him when he comes out of hiding. Bath indeed!

CELLINI. I expect he's a bit tied up at the moment. Well, good-bye.
Mrs. Abbott. *Arrivederci.*

(*There are sudden bumps from the bathroom and muffled shouts.*)

KATE. What's that?

CELLINI. Is Mr. Abbott.

KATE. He doesn't usually make noises like that. Don't say we've caught another curate! There are a terrible lot about this year.

> (*She goes towards the bathroom again and* CELLINI *gets fidgety and puts his hand in his pocket, feeling for his gun. The front door-bell rings.*) (*Crossing to the front door.*) Really, this place is like a belfry today. Ding, dong. Ding, dong.

> (*She opens the front door and in steps the* BURGLAR *in yet another disguise. This time he is a policeman in a skin-tight uniform with a very large helmet and another moustache.*)

BURGLAR. Good afternoon, miss. (*He does the classic policeman's knees-bend.*)

KATE. Oh, good afternoon—er—officer. (*She almost does it back.*)

BURGLAR. I wonder if I might 'ave a few words with you. I 'ave reason to believe there's a burglar in the area.

> (*He crosses to* C., *followed by* KATE.)

KATE. Why, yes, that's right. He was here a little while ago dressed up as a postman. I meant to report it, but so many things have happened since.

BURGLAR. Yus, well, per'aps I could 'ave a look round for clues. I'll try to keep it as short as possible.

KATE. That's what they seem to have done to your uniform. You don't really think he's still here, do you? The burglar, I mean.

BURGLAR. 'E may be closer than you think!

KATE (*looking at him closely*). Are you sure we haven't met before some-where? Your face seems very familiar.

BURGLAR (*pulling his helmet down low*). You must be thinking of me bruvver. 'E sells nylons in Oxford Street. Now then. (*Pointing to bathroom.*) What's in there?

> (*All this while* CELLINI *has been edging stealthily towards the door and is at this precise moment tip-toeing up the steps when the* BURGLAR *turns and spots him.*)

Aha! (*Knees bend.*)

CELLINI. Aha! (*Knees bend.*)

> (*They bob up and down at one another until interrupted by more bumps from the bathroom.*)

KATE. There it is again. Oh. (*Hand to mouth.*) Perhaps it's the burglar.

CELLINI. Nonsense. Is Mr. Abbott.

BURGLAR (*with genuine interest*). Does 'e live in there?

KATE. Don't you think we ought to look?

BURGLAR. Well, I—er—yes. No 'arm in looking, I suppose. Unless 'e's shy.

> (*The* BURGLAR *advances towards the bathroom. He is followed by* KATE, *who is followed by* CELLINI, *who has taken out his gun in*

desperation. *Suddenly the* BURGLAR *turns round on* KATE, *who turns round to find herself facing the gun.*)

KATE (*screams*). A gun!

BURGLAR. Cor stone the crows!

CELLINI (*to* BURGLAR). Kindly put your 'ands up.

    (*The* BURGLAR *does so, but as* CELLINI *steps towards him,* KATE *picks up the vase containing the necklace, creeps up behind him and breaks it over his head. The vase shatters,* CELLINI *falls to the ground unconscious and the necklace drops out at the* BURGLAR'S *feet.*)

BURGLAR. 'Ooray! Well bowled! 'Allo, you dropped your beads. (*He picks them up, but takes a closer look.*) 'Arf a minute, though.

KATE. However did those get in there?

BURGLAR. I'll take care of these. (*He stuffs them into his helmet and puts it on again.*)

KATE (*looking at* CELLINI). Do you think I've killed him?

BURGLAR (*very casual about it all*). No. You gave 'im a right fourpenny one, though. 'E's out cold. (*He takes possession of* CELLINI'S *gun.*) Well, 'e won't need this.

KATE. Shouldn't we pour water over him or something?

BURGLAR. What and ruin my getaway—er—'is suit, I mean? Not likely. Well, I'd best be going. (*He moves towards the door.*)

KATE (*indicating* CELLINI). But what about this? Aren't you going to arrest him or anything?

BURGLAR. What time is it?

KATE. About six o'clock.

BURGLAR. Oh well, then I'm off duty. Sorry. Ta ta!

    (*He goes out, to the accompaniment of more bumps from the bathroom.* KATE *rushes to the door.*)

KATE. Hey! What about the thing in the bathroom?

    (*But it's too late, the* BURGLAR *has gone.*)

Ohhh!

    (*More bumps from the bathroom and she rushes over and shouts at the door.*)

David! Be quiet!

    (*More bumps.* CELLINI *groans and sits up. She runs back to him and hits him with a tray.*)

And you!

    (*He subsides.* KATE *picks up the umbrella from the sofa, advances to the bathroom and unlocks the door.*)

Now come on out!

    (DAVID *and* MARIA, *still tied together, come staggering out like Siamese twins.*)

Oh no, not again! I thought I could trust you two together by now. What have you got to say for yourself this time?

>(DAVID *makes grunting noises behind the gag until* KATE *lets him out.*)

DAVID. Phew! Thanks, old girl.

>(MARIA *collapses on to the couch.*)

MARIA. Thank 'eaven. That was terrible. (*To* DAVID.) You need a shave.

KATE. Now, what's all this about?

DAVID. Well, you'll never believe this, but you know that chap Cellini? (*He spots him on the floor.*) Oh there he is. What's he doing down there?

MARIA (*hopefully*). Is 'e dead?

KATE. No, just asleep. I hit him with a vase. It was most satisfying. Come and give me a hand with him.

DAVID. How the devil can I? (*He turns and shows her his tied hands.*)

KATE. My sheets! Oh, David, how could you?

DAVID. I didn't do it! Who do you think I am—Houdini?

>(KATE *unties* DAVID, *who releases* MARIA.)

MARIA. Well, at least he didn't get the necklace.

KATE. Is that the one the policeman took with him?

DAVID. What?

MARIA. The police 'ave been 'ere?

KATE. Yes, a funny little man who— (*Hand to mouth.*) Oh! I've just remembered who he was. I thought he was familiar.

DAVID. Why, what did he do?

KATE. No, I mean I thought I recognized his face. It was the burglar again.

MARIA (*wailing*). And 'e 'as got ze diamonds!

DAVID. Oh Lord! Not again!

>(*The door-bell rings and* DAVID *opens the door. Enter* MRS. SCOTT *with the* BURGLAR *dressed as before. She propels him in by giving him an efficient half-nelson. She is carrying his helmet by the strap in her other hand.*)

MRS. SCOTT. Thank you, David dear. I've brought you a visitor. I found it out in the street.

KATE. } (*together*). That's him.
MARIA. }

MRS. SCOTT. Oh, you know him, do you? He seems a very nasty piece of work to me. I asked him if he'd seen anything of Mr. Cellini and he said a very rude word. So, of course, I knew he wasn't a real constable. Besides, look at his boots.

BURGLAR. Wot about me boots?

MRS. SCOTT. Size sixes! I never saw a policeman with small feet.

KATE. Better look out, Mother, he's got a gun.

MRS. SCOTT. No, he hasn't. I've got it.

> (*She takes it out of the helmet and flourishes it.*)

BURGLAR. Lady, please don't wave it about like that. It might go orf.

MRS. SCOTT. You sit down there and keep quiet!

> (*She pushes him into the chair by the bathroom, stepping over* CELLINI *on the way.*)

Excuse me. Oh, there you are. I wondered where you'd got to.

DAVID. But how on earth did you tackle him?

MRS. SCOTT. Judo, dear. Evening classes. You ought to go in for it. It would do you the world of good and get rid of that tummy. Much better for you than learning Russian.

DAVID. But I'm not learning Russian.

MRS. SCOTT. Then it's a waste of time taking lessons.

KATE. Mother, you're marvellous!

BURGLAR. That's a matter of opinion!

MRS. SCOTT. You speak when you're spoken to or I'll give you a Boston Crab! (*She advances threateningly towards him.*)

BURGLAR. Keep 'er orf! She's already cockled me truncheon.

MRS. SCOTT. No spirit. That's the trouble with this generation. Look at his ears.

BURGLAR. You're very rude, aren't yer? Wot's wrong wiv me ears?

MRS. SCOTT. Higher than your eyes. A very bad sign. Criminal type. (*She indicates* CELLINI.) Must he sleep on the floor? It's very draughty and rather inconvenient.

DAVID (*who has been feeling his own ears and finds one is higher than the other*). He's a smuggler.

MRS. SCOTT. Oh really? Been drinking his own brandy, I suppose. What a good thing he's not really your boy-friend, Maria. You might have had to live in a cave.

MARIA. 'Ow do you know 'e is not Carlo?

MRS. SCOTT. Woman's intuition, my dear. His name's in his hat.

DAVID. The question is, what are we going to do with him now?

MRS. SCOTT. Oh, we can take him along with us.

KATE. Along where?

MRS. SCOTT. To the police station, of course. I asked Mrs. Mac-Whatsit to phone for a police car to collect him— (*She jerks her thumb at the* BURGLAR.)

BURGLAR. Thanks very much!

MRS. SCOTT. I dare say they'll have room for an extra one or else they can stuff him in the boot. I told you the police always have big boots. By the way, this fell out of his helmet. Pretty, isn't it? (*She takes the necklace out of the helmet and holds it up.*)

BURGLAR. That's mine.

Mrs. Scott. You be quiet or I'll show you the Irish Whip!
Burglar. No, no. Anything but the whip!
            (Mrs. Scott *examines the necklace.*)
Mrs. Scott. Worth a pound or two, I dare say.
David. A pound or two!
Mrs. Scott. Well, it's extremely well done. One of the best imitations I've seen.
        (*The only one who doesn't react unfavourably to this announcement is* Maria.)
Burglar. Wot?
David. You mean they aren't real?
Mrs. Scott. Of course not. Just glass.
Kate. Oh, what a pity. They look gorgeous.
Cellini (*sitting up*). I am being swindled!
Kate. You be quiet! (*She hits him again with the tray and he subsides.*)
Burglar. False pretences, that's what it is. It ain't honest!
David. But I don't understand. If they're only glass, then—
Maria. Then I am not a smuggler, after all, eh?
David. No, I suppose not. Then why did Cellini—
Maria (*lightly*). Per'aps someone did ze double-cross, after all, eh?
  (*She looks inexpressibly innocent.*)
David (*doubtfully*). Er-yes.
Mrs. Scott. Well, I'd better hand it over to the police, anyway.
        (Mrs. MacWhimble *appears at the door with two* Policemen.)
Mrs. Mac. That's 'im.
Mrs. Scott. Just in time. May I see your boots, please, officers?
        (*They are a little nonplussed, but do as they are asked, one foot after the other, like chorus-girls in slow motion.*)
First-class! We have two of them for you. There they are.
1st Policeman (*moving to* Burglar *while the other kneels by* Cellini).
  What's the charge, indecent exposure?
David. False pretences.
Kate. Breaking and entering.
Mrs. Mac. Kicking up a rumpus in the 'all. (*She stalks out.*)
1st Policeman. Right you are. The Sergeant would like a few words with you, my lad.
Burglar. I don't get no luck at all. I should 'ave stuck to the old three-card trick.
        (David *sprays* Cellini *with the soda siphon to bring him round.*)
David. Wakey, wakey!
            (Cellini *sits up gasping.*)
2nd Policeman. What about this one, then?
David (*handing over* Cellini's *stick*). How about possessing a sword-stick without a licence?

2ND POLICEMAN. That'll do to be getting on with. (*He hauls* CELLINI *to his feet.*) Come on, you!

1ST POLICEMAN (*moving to the door and addressing* MRS. SCOTT). Thanks for the tip, ma'am. Perhaps you would come down to the station and make a statement.

MRS. SCOTT. Of course. Good-bye, Kate dear. (*She kisses her.*) Good-bye, David. Remember what I said about judo. Oh, Maria, do write and tell me when you get married, I'm sure you'll be very happy. (*Kisses Maria. To* 1ST POLICEMAN.) Come along, I want a word with you about your ridiculous parking regulations.

(*She sweeps out with the* 1ST POLICEMAN *and the* BURGLAR.)

MARIA. I go, too.

DAVID. What, now?

MARIA. Yes, David. Is best I go. (*To* 2ND POLICEMAN.) Can you drive me to the station?

2ND POLICEMAN. It'd be a pleasure, miss. Do you want to make a statement, too?

MARIA. No. I want to catch a train. I go before anything else 'appen. Good-bye, Mrs. Abbott—Katie. Take care of 'im.

KATE. Don't worry, I will. Good-bye!

DAVID. Good-bye.

MARIA (*looking round wistfully*). Maybe I come back one day for ze real 'oliday, yes?

DAVID. By jove, yes! (*Seeing* KATE's *expression.*) That's to say, well, maybe!

2ND POLICEMAN (*moving to the door with* CELLINI *in tow*). Coming, miss?

MARIA. *Si*, per'aps you will take my cases.

2ND POLICEMAN (*to* CELLINI). C'mon, you. Make yourself useful. Carry the lady's bags downstairs.

(CELLINI *picks up the two suitcases.*)

DAVID. And don't forget your hat!

(*He jams it down hard over* CELLINI's *head and, still in a daze,* CELLINI *staggers out with the two cases, closely followed by the* 2ND POLICEMAN.)

MARIA (*going towards the door*). I will write when I get 'ome, David.

DAVID. Er—good show.

MARIA. Only zis time I write in English, eh? Oh, and, David?

DAVID. Yes?

MARIA. Don't worry about ze *real* necklace. Is quite safe.

DAVID. But—

MARIA. *Arrivederci*, David. (*She kisses him. A long, lingering kiss which leaves him glassy-eyed.*) Per'aps we meet again one day.

(*Exit* MARIA.)

KATE. Well, that's that. If you're sure you can tear yourself away.

DAVID (*who has been standing looking out of the empty doorway*). Eh? Oh, yes. You know I can't help thinking that girl takes after her father. (*He closes the door and stands looking fondly at* KATE *for a moment. He holds out his arms to her.*) Darling!

KATE. Not so fast, young man. I haven't forgiven you yet.

DAVID. Oh, come on, darling. Fainites! (*He holds out his hands with fingers crossed.*)

(KATE *considers for a moment with her head on one side then breaks into a laugh and runs into his arms.*)

KATE. Darling!

(*They kiss.*)

DAVID. Happy?

KATE. Hmmm!

(*He leads her to the couch, where she sits. Then solemnly he goes to the bathroom door and turns the "Engaged" sign over. It now reads "Just Married". Without a word he turns on the lamp and comes to sit beside* KATE *on the couch. He puts his arm slowly round her.*)

DAVID. Now, Mrs. Abbott. Where were we?

(*He goes to kiss her, but she puts a finger to his lips.*)

KATE. Music, darling. Give me atmosphere.

(DAVID, *without really looking, reaches out and puts on the first record which comes to hand.*)

Something romantic.

(*They fall into one another's arms as the record starts. It is the Linguaphone lesson which* DAVID *was using at the beginning of Act One and the voice sounds remarkably like* MARIA'*s.*)

KATE *screams with exasperation as*

THE CURTAIN FALLS

FURNITURE AND PROPERTY PLOT

ACT I

On stage

Easy chair (D.L.)

Studio couch
    On it: DAVID's collar and tie

Coffee table (by couch)
    On it: Record player with Italian
    record

Small table (behind couch)
    On it: Table-lamp
    Telephone

Vacuum cleaner (plugged into table-lamp)

Sideboard (U.L.)
    On it: Various wine-bottles, full
    and half-full
    Soda syphon
    Wine and brandy glasses
    Cigar box containing buttons
    Feather duster
    Transistor radio
    In the drawer: Tack hammer
    Tacks
    Pencil

Umbrella stand (left of front door)
    In it: One gentleman's umbrella

Book case (U.R.)
    On it: Empty wine bottle
    Table runner
    Knitting needles and wool
    Cardboard notice: "Out of
    Order—Please Use the Bell"
    Crayon
    India rubber
    Books and papers

Dining table (D.R.)
    On it: Tablecloth and remnants of
    a meal

Four dining chairs to match (three
    by table and one between bathroom and bedroom)

Three pictures ("Psyche" nearest
    front door; "Dante and Beatrice"
    by bedroom; "Monarch of the
    Glen" D.L.)

"Engaged/Just Married" notice (on
    bathroom door)

Carpets and rugs

Window curtains and pelmet

Cushions, L.P. record covers, magazines and papers (on couch, chairs
    and floor)

Vases and ornaments

In bathroom: Bathroom chair

In bedroom: Small wardrobe

Offstage

In bathroom: Powder and puff (KATE)
    Sports jacket (DAVID)

In bedroom: Small suitcase (KATE)
    Bottle of Italian brandy (MARIA)
    Bath robe
    Bath towel   } (MARIA)
    Washing bag

In kitchen: Broken kettle (DAVID)

By front door: Two large suit-cases
    (TAXI DRIVER)
    Collecting tin (CURATE)

Personal

KATE: Small apron
    In the pocket: Two dusters

DAVID: Wrist watch
    Italian phrase book

MRS. MACWHIMBLE: Copy of lease

MRS. SCOTT: Handbag
    Gloves

MARIA: Handbag
    In it: Packet of diamonds
    Small note book
    Wad of £1 notes

TAXI DRIVER: 2s. 6d. change in
    trousers pocket

ACT II

Scene 1

Strike: Cleaner

Set

  On couch: Large pillows, sheets and two blankets made up into a bed
  By couch: Maria's slippers
  On coffee table: Book for Mrs. Scott

Move: Coffee table to R. of couch

Off stage

  In bathroom: Small blanket (DAVID)
  In kitchen: Glass of milk (MARIA)

  Glass of milk (DAVID)
  Car rug (MARIA)
Front door: Sword-stick (CELLINI)
  Large poker (MRS. MACWHIMBLE)

Personal

  DAVID: Handkerchief
  MARIA: Handbag
    In it: Packet of diamonds
  BURGLAR: Mask
    Gun
    Cap
  CELLINI: White scarf

Scene 2

Strike: "Psyche"

Set

  On table: Breakfast for four with plates, cups and saucers, knives, egg spoons, tea spoons, coffee and tea pots, burnt toast, plate of eggs, marmalade and lump sugar

  By table: Large tray

  On couch: Fold bed-clothes into a neat pile

Off stage

  In kitchen: Jug of milk (KATE)
    Plate of watercress sandwiches (MRS. SCOTT)
  In bedroom: Underclothes (MARIA)
  Front door: Plumber's bag
    In it: Plumber's tools including a large suction stick (MRS. BOTTLE)

Personal

  MRS. SCOTT: Knitting
  CURATE: Clerical hat
    Pince-nez

ACT III

Strike

  Breakfast things from table
  David's pyjamas and dressing gown

Set

  On sideboard: Watercress sandwiches
    Brandy bottle
  On coffee table: Breakable vase
    Tin tray
  On couch: Tearable sheets
  On easy chair: Newspaper

Check: Feather duster on sideboard
  Cigar-box with buttons on sideboard

Restore bathroom door and re-hang "Engaged" notice

Tidy room

Off stage

  In bathroom: Tea-towel (DAVID)
  In bedroom: Two suitcases (MARIA)
    Clothing (MARIA)

  In kitchen: Shopping basket (KATE)

  Front door: Brick in a parcel (POST-MAN)
    Registration slip (POSTMAN)
    Empty mail-bag (POSTMAN)
    Shopping (KATE)
    Sword-stick (CELLINI)

Personal

  DAVID: Roll of Polo-mints
    Box of matches
  MRS. MACWHIMBLE: Notice to quit
    Packet containing diamond necklace
  POSTMAN: Gun
  CELLINI: Silk scarf
    Gun
    Cigar-case with cigars
    Ornate lighter
    Cigarettes (*not* filter-tipped)